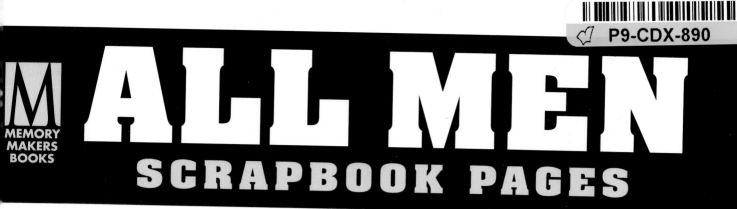

ALL MEN
SCRAPBOOK PAGES

MEMORY MAKERS BOOKS

Fireman's Prayer

When I'm called to duty God wherever flames may rage,
give me the strength to save some life whatever be it age.
Help me embrace a little child Before its too late,
or save an older person from the horror of that fate.
Enable me to be alert and hear the weakest shout,
and quickly and effeciently to put the fire out.
I want to fill my calling and to give the best in me,
to guard my every neighbor and protect their property.
And if according to your will I do lose my life,
please bless with Your Protective Hand,
my children and my wife.

HERO

HERO

INVENTIVE IDEAS FOR MASCULINE LAYOUTS

MANAGING EDITOR MaryJo Regier

EDITOR Emily Curry Hitchingham

ART DIRECTOR Nick Nyffeler

GRAPHIC DESIGNERS Jordan Kinney, Robin Rozum

ART ACQUISITIONS EDITOR Janetta Abucejo Wieneke

CRAFT EDITOR Jodi Amidei

PHOTOGRAPHER Ken Trujillo

CONTRIBUTING PHOTOGRAPHERS Lizzy Creazo, Jennifer Reeves

CONTRIBUTING WRITER Heather A. Eades

EDITORIAL SUPPORT Karen Cain, Amy Glander, Dena Twinem

CONTRIBUTING MEMORY MAKERS MASTERS Jessie Baldwin, Valerie Barton, Joanna Bolick, Christine Brown, Sheila Doherty, Kathy Fesmire, Nic Howard, Julie Johnson, Kelli Noto, Torrey Scott, Shannon Taylor, Andrea Lyn Vetten-Marley, Samantha Walker, Holle Wiktorek

Published by Memory Makers Books, an imprint of F+W Publications, Inc.
12365 Huron Street, Suite 500, Denver, CO 80234
Phone (800) 254-9124
First edition. Printed in the United States.
09 08 07 06 05   5 4 3 2 1

Library of Congress Cataloging-in-Publication Data

All men scrapbook pages : inventive ideas for masculine layouts.--1st ed.
     p. cm.
  Includes index.
  ISBN 1-892127-67-9
  1. Photograph albums. 2. Scrapbooks. 3. Photography of men.

TR501.A45 2005
745.593--dc22   2005052225

Distributed to trade and art markets by
F+W Publications, Inc.
4700 East Galbraith Road, Cincinnati, OH 45236
Phone (800) 289-0963
ISBN 1-892127-67-9

Distributed in Canada by Fraser Direct
100 Armstrong Avenue
Georgetown, ON, Canada L7G 5S4
Tel: (905) 877-4411

Distributed in the U.K. and Europe by David & Charles
Brunel House, Newton Abbot, Devon, TQ12 4PU, England
Tel: (+44) 1626 323200, Fax: (+44) 1626 323319
E-mail: mail@davidandcharles.co.uk

Distributed in Australia by Capricorn Link
P.O. Box 704, S. Windsor NSW, 2756 Australia
Tel: (02) 4577-3555

Memory Makers Books is the home of *Memory Makers*, the scrapbook magazine dedicated to educating and inspiring scrapbookers. To subscribe, or for more information, call (800) 366-6465.
Visit us on the Internet at www.memorymakersmagazine.com.

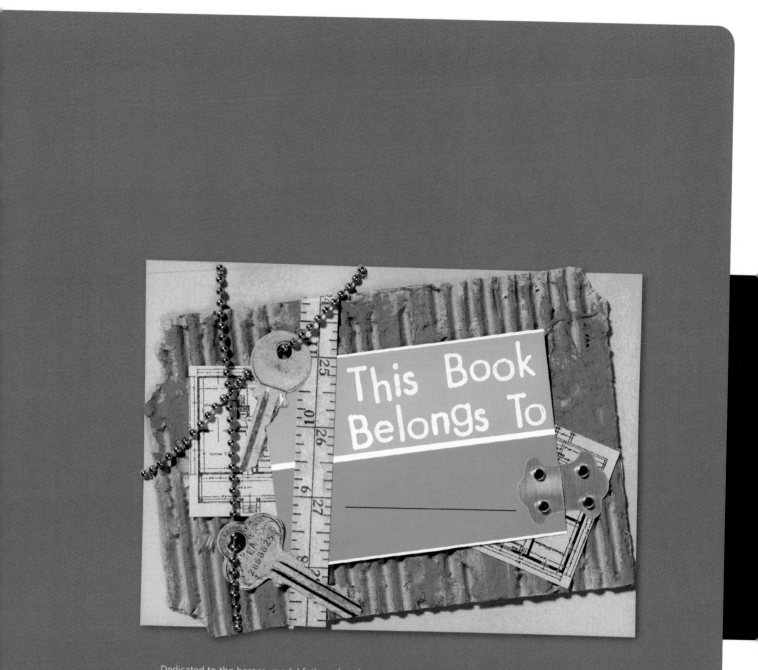

This Book
Belongs To

_____

Dedicated to the heroes, model fathers, handymen, Mr. Rights, beloved grandpas, better halves, sports nuts, favorite uncles, outdoorsmen and kid brothers that inspired the scrapbook pages inside.

TABLE OF CONTENTS

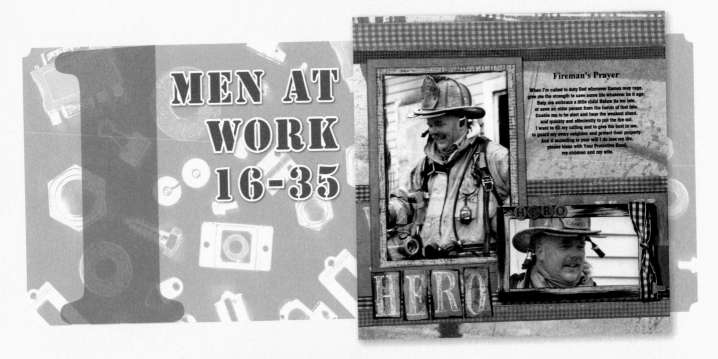

FAMILY GUYS 60-83

Brothers

Extra Tough

50% Pals
30% Loyal
20% Rivals

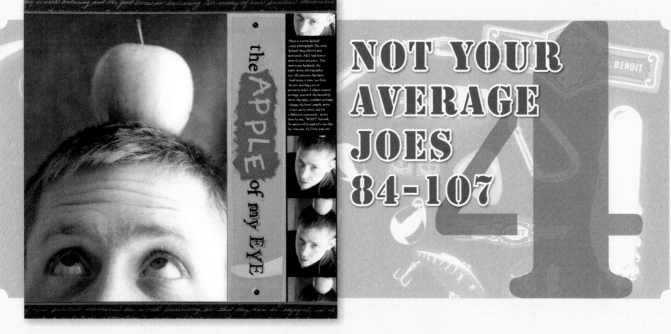

NOT YOUR AVERAGE JOES 84-107

If you have been looking for artistic ways to take the testosterone factor up a notch in your masculine scrapbook pages, this is the idea resource you've been waiting for. After all, why should masculine layouts look the same as any others in your albums? Man-powered pages call for treatments as unique as the men they feature. With that in mind, we created *All Men Scrapbook Pages* to take the guesswork out of designing distinctive scrapbook pages that reflect the facets of men's lives using the latest looks and products.

To help you create unmistakably male-oriented layouts, we've filled this book chock-full with fun and innovative ideas sure to set your creative wheels turning at a fast and furious pace. We start off with a sampling of clever ideas for getting men involved in the pages that feature them (it can in fact be done!) along with a comprehensive look at design choices and page additions that pack the most punch possible into your man pages. With your imagination warmed up and ready to go, you'll be all set to launch into the collection of outstanding pages to come, which include men and their careers, pastimes, families and much more. In all, this compilation is the ultimate one-stop resource for jump-starting page ideas that will streak past the finish line with flying colors.

With this book, we encourage you to break from the confines and comfort zones that until now may have defined your masculine pages. Men are larger than life and should therefore be celebrated in pages that speak to their personalities and personal tastes. So put away those gender-neutral papers and page accents for another project. You're in man territory now—think big, think bold and, above all, think MASCULINE!

Enjoy,

Emily

Emily Curry Hitchingham, Associate Editor

Paul – so many adjectives come to mind when I think of trying to describe him; strong, kind, generous, honest, loyal, intelligent, caring...the list could go on and on. He has been such a constant in our lives, always there as a friend and a confidant. He's been though the tough times with us, and the all the good times. He has always been supportive and offered his help when we needed it the most. I am so thankful that he found his soul mate that he searched so hard to find. No one deserves to be happier than this wonderful man; he deserves it all!

GETTING MEN INVOLVED

As with any scrapbook page, a willing subject makes for the most endearing and authentic pages. With the right approach, you'll discover how painless it can be to get the special men in your life to play a small role in the creation of the scrapbook pages that feature them. Still skeptical? Simply come to the craft table with one of the game plans below and soon you'll be scoring exceptional pages that were the result of a team effort.

Amy Goldstein, Kent Lakes, New York

AFTER THE STORM

Talking With a Scrapbook Widower

It's a common tale among husbands of scrappers that they are neglected, so we decided to have a chat with one personally to see how he is surviving "**The Paper Storm.**"

We asked Jeff what it was like spending all those Saturday nights alone on the couch and he responded with a resolute,"I was a long cold winter this year but summer is looking more promising. I might even get her out of the house this weekend."

When asked what he likes to do while his wife is busy in her "cave" (as he refers to her art studio), he replied, "Alas, if she won't give me any attention, I can at least retire to the porch and have a good cigar and a glass of wine by myself.",

What about the Children?

"The kids and I look longingly at pictures of her from the era that was pre-scrapping and fondly remember those times."

What do you see for the future?

"Well, hopefully, she will come up for air soon and I can get her away from computer and we can have a hot meal!"

2005

INTERVIEWS

No doubt your inquiring mind wants to know what makes your man tick. And who doesn't enjoy feeling like a bit of a celebrity from time to time? Your man is a multifaceted, news-worthy personality. Make sure you get the exclusive scoop with a series of fun or more serious-minded questions and include what you uncover in a layout.

Amy's husband was more than happy to oblige his wife and put in his two cents on her scrapbooking "obsession"—a pastime which he playfully (albeit woefully) refers to as Amy's "time away" from the family. And because Amy's tongue-in-cheek approach suited his taste for sarcasm, her husband was especially enthusiastic, making for a fun end result.

QUESTIONNAIRES

Supply your man with a short series of questions for him to personally answer that speak to his interests, character, personality and perspectives. You can repeat his answers in journaling elements you create, or you may wish to craft a customized form to incorporate into your page design. Either way you'll end up with insights that came straight from his heart.

After seeing this photo of her husband, Shannon was struck by how it captured the mature and fatherly side of his personality. Although she initially amassed a list of questions for him to answer in her notebook, she soon found her man responded better to addressing each one aloud while she wrote down his responses. In fact, as her husband elaborated and grew more enthusiastic, Shannon soon found herself scrambling to keep up!

Shannon Taylor, Bristol, Tennessee

HANDWRITTEN JOURNALING

Having your man pen the journaling for a page is an easy and exceptional way to document his one-of-a-kind handwriting and perspective. You may wish to provide him with the journaling element you'd like to use in your design, such as a select kind and size of paper, card or tag. Or, you can leave it up to his devices to determine the format he sees fit. For personal sentiments, consider incorporating the journaling into some kind of hidden element to be revealed selectively.

Heather knew she wanted to design a layout devoted to the special relationship her husband and daughter share. Because writing is something her husband enjoys, having him scribe his own tender sentiments toward daughter Kiersten made the most sense—and made for a wonderful contribution to the page the family can reflect back on in the years ahead. In fact, Heather's husband's "assignment" ultimately spurred a touching father-daughter moment. While walking past her home office, she caught a glimpse of her husband reading his recently penned note to the little girl who inspired it.

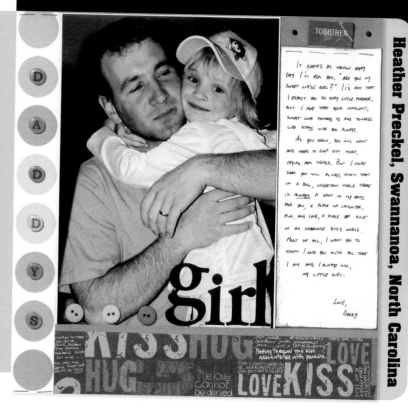

Heather Preckel, Swannanoa, North Carolina

Courtney Walsh, Winnebago, Illinois

PHOTO DIARIES

Although this approach requires more of a commitment on his part, you'll be surprised to see the enthusiasm that ensues once his creative wheels start turning. Hand the camera over to your man with the objective that he chronicle a scrapbook-worthy subject from his perspective. Simply set him loose and see what photos and supporting journaling he returns with, then scrapbook them for an especially meaningful man page.

Courtney's husband, Adam, had strong feelings about what he wanted to document—special early-morning alone time with their youngest child, Ethan. Even as Courtney began work on the page design, Adam couldn't help but jump in and add his input (it turns out it was Adam's idea to include the cropped photos in the journaling element). In addition to discovering what her two men do in the early hours of the day, Courtney learned it can be helpful to have her husband's perspective on her page design!

So what makes one man page stall and another streak past the finish line with flying colors? There are several ways you can fine-tune your masculine layouts in order to turn out a high-performance page each and every time. Try your hand at detailing your designs with these distinctive tips, tricks and techniques.

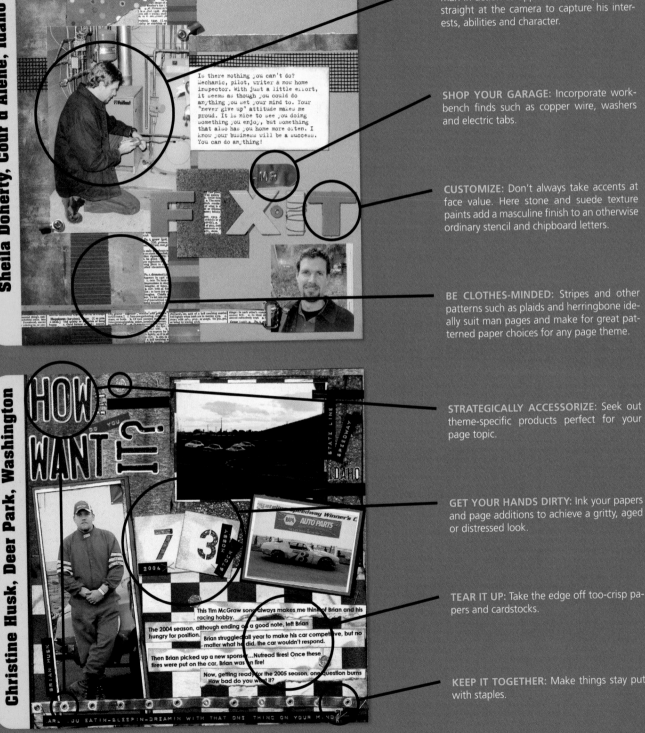

GET INTO THE ACT: Snap shots of your man in action as opposed to always smiling straight at the camera to capture his interests, abilities and character.

SHOP YOUR GARAGE: Incorporate workbench finds such as copper wire, washers and electric tabs.

CUSTOMIZE: Don't always take accents at face value. Here stone and suede texture paints add a masculine finish to an otherwise ordinary stencil and chipboard letters.

BE CLOTHES-MINDED: Stripes and other patterns such as plaids and herringbone ideally suit man pages and make for great patterned paper choices for any page theme.

STRATEGICALLY ACCESSORIZE: Seek out theme-specific products perfect for your page topic.

GET YOUR HANDS DIRTY: Ink your papers and page additions to achieve a gritty, aged or distressed look.

TEAR IT UP: Take the edge off too-crisp papers and cardstocks.

KEEP IT TOGETHER: Make things stay put with staples.

Sheila Doherty, Cour d'Alene, Idaho

Christine Husk, Deer Park, Washington

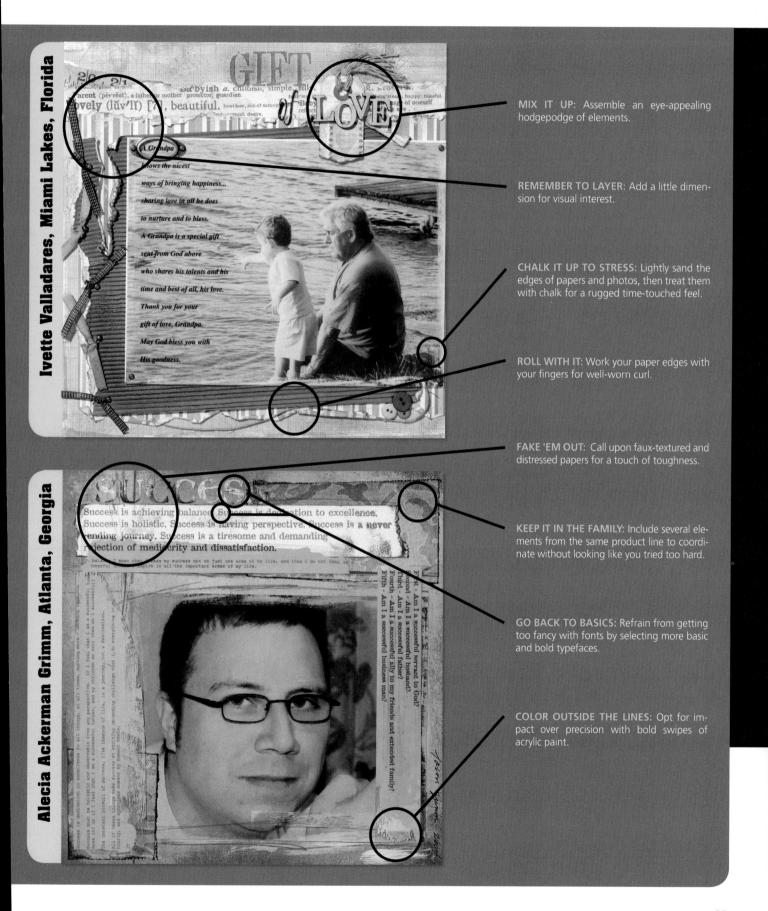

Ivette Valladares, Miami Lakes, Florida

GIFT of LOVE

A Grandpa knows the nicest ways of bringing happiness... sharing love in all he does to nurture and to bless. A Grandpa is a special gift sent from God above who shares his talents and his time and best of all, his love. Thank you for your gift of love, Grandpa. May God bless you with His goodness.

MIX IT UP: Assemble an eye-appealing hodgepodge of elements.

REMEMBER TO LAYER: Add a little dimension for visual interest.

CHALK IT UP TO STRESS: Lightly sand the edges of papers and photos, then treat them with chalk for a rugged time-touched feel.

ROLL WITH IT: Work your paper edges with your fingers for well-worn curl.

FAKE 'EM OUT: Call upon faux-textured and distressed papers for a touch of toughness.

KEEP IT IN THE FAMILY: Include several elements from the same product line to coordinate without looking like you tried too hard.

GO BACK TO BASICS: Refrain from getting too fancy with fonts by selecting more basic and bold typefaces.

COLOR OUTSIDE THE LINES: Opt for impact over precision with bold swipes of acrylic paint.

Alecia Ackerman Grimm, Atlanta, Georgia

Success

Success is achieving balance. Success is dedication to excellence. Success is holistic. Success is having perspective. Success is a never-ending journey. Success is a tiresome and demanding rejection of mediocrity and dissatisfaction.

MUSCLE-ADDING PAGE ELEMENTS

While there certainly exists a soft side to even the most strapping of male personalities, it is hard to resist pulling out all the stops when it comes to man-powered pages. When gender-neutral papers and page additions just won't do the job, turn up the testosterone factor by detailing your layouts with some of the following products.

STENCILS: *Pump up the look of letters and numbers with the use of stencils, whether you adorn and incorporate the actual stencil itself, use only the punch-out portion or paint or ink the page with them the old-fashioned way.*

OFFICE SUPPLIES: *Document his day job with around-the-office-inspired elements such as reproduction binder clips, file folders, folio closures, label holders, labels and paper clips for a little 9 to 5 flair.*

STENCILS

OFFICE SUPPLIES

MESH

HARDWARE

PAINT CHIPS

MESH: *Metal and traditional mesh reminiscent of screen doors and windows, chain-link fence and drywall tape are perfect for adding a little texture and tool-time chic into masculine designs.*

HARDWARE: *What would a man page be without the nuts and bolts? No screwdrivers and hammers are required for toughening up a page embellished with hinges, hangers, hooks and brads that look as though they were supplied straight from the toolbox.*

PAINT CHIPS: *Pack a punch of color into your man page with the simple (and cost-free) addition of paint chips.*

AUTO ACCENTS: *Is your man going places? Pay homage to his sense of adventure with the freewheeling look of faux tires, tracks and customized plates that require no registration.*

BOTTLE CAPS: *Flattened cans may never find their way onto a scrapbook page, but flattened bottle caps certainly have. Add these authentic little remnants that look as though your man really did leave them behind to refresh any page design.*

WOVEN LABELS: *Men are far too unique to be one-size-fits-all, but clever woven clothes labels and sentiments can size up their qualities and characteristics with style.*

LEATHER: *The innate toughness of leather doesn't limit it to tough guy themes. Dimension and richness can instantly be added with the use of leather frames and embossed accents.*

LAMINATE CHIPS: *Improve layouts of any theme with these home improvement store samples.*

GAME PIECES: *Do you have a joker or a king of hearts on your hands? Playing cards and game pieces such as Scrabble letters, dominoes and puzzle pieces play up the fun-loving nature of any boy at heart while providing a punch of pizazz to a page.*

WATCH PARTS: *Incorporate elements of Father Time such as watch parts for a timeless, distinguished look.*

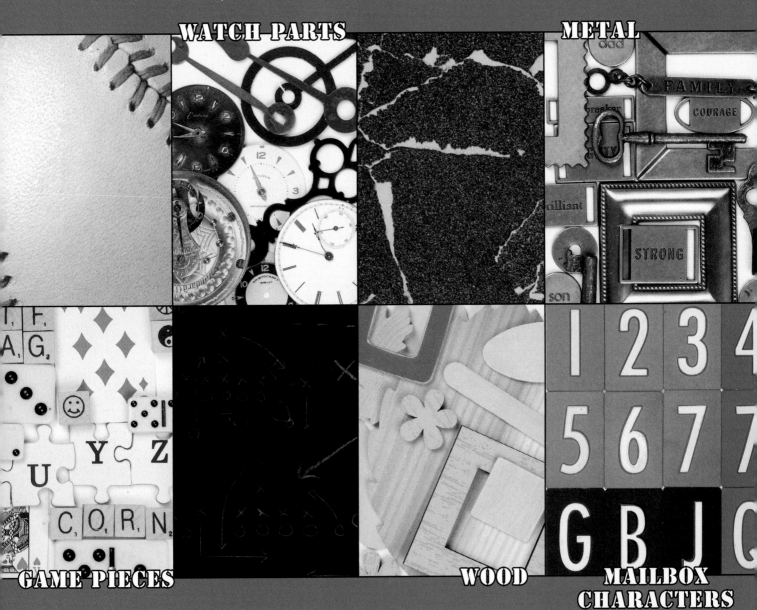

WATCH PARTS

METAL

GAME PIECES

WOOD

MAILBOX CHARACTERS

WOOD: *Nothing adds brawn to a page quite like a little timber. Wooden embellishments work in designs that are both rough and rugged or sophisticated and refined and may be painted, distressed or left au naturel.*

METAL: *Few elements enhance masculine-themed pages the way metal can. This material can connote a sense of sleekness or conjure up a strong, industrial feel. Look to items like washer words, frames, chains, keys, ribbon charms and the like to meld an ideal design together.*

MAILBOX CHARACTERS: *Commemorate your king of the castle with the bold and unmistakable look of mailbox characters and digits.*

CHIPBOARD: *Frames, letters and coasters comprised of this sturdy material add a bit of heft to any manly design without adding a lot of bulk.*

DIE CUTS: *For every guy's guy activity and interest there exists a die cut to immortalize it. Re-create the look of the real thing in the form of these page-ready accents.*

CHIPBOARD

BUTTONS

DIE CUTS

STICKERS

PRINTED SENTIMENTS

STICKERS: *A far cry from your average page add-ons, canvas-style, photo, vintage-themed and word stickers can be put to work on any man page.*

BUTTONS: *Mimic the look of cuff links, military uniforms and his favorite button-down shirt with the addition of strategically chosen notions for a finishing touch.*

PRINTED SENTIMENTS: *Say it plain and simple with preprinted page accents.*

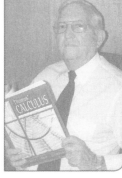

1

MEN AT WORK

When it comes to earning wages, your man navigates the work world the best way he knows how—*his* way. No doubt his aptitude and attitude have won him a role in a vocation for which he should be proud. Herald the achievements of your everyday hero in your scrapbooks to show him you appreciate his efforts. After all, he works hard for the money—so you better treat him right!

Amy Goldstein, Kent Lakes, New York

{Volunteer} Fire Fighter

S ome men & women choose to put their life on the line and help others as a profession. And then there are those who choose to do it voluntarily and for no monetary compensation; on top of their chosen careers. These brave souls are VOLUNTEER fire fighters.

Most volunteer firefighters, carry a one-way pager which goes off whenever there is a call. They listen to the "tones" as they are called, then go to their car to join the other firefighters on the call. When they are at the fire station, they constantly check apparatuses, trucks and equipment to make sure things are working properly. "We turn on all equipment such as lights, pumps, sirens and radios and if something is broken we mark it, take it out of service and get it repaired." said one volunteer.

Fire calls er grass or forest fires, house fires (or other type of buildings, example: barns), or car fires. Each involves different techniques and equipment to handle. They also respond to calls to assist other fire departments in our area; which called mutual aid.

In addition, a great deal of time is spent raising money for the fire department. This is an integral part of the job. This helps to keep our station operational and the firemen in workable equipment.

The day can be long and monotonous with little appreciation from the public but the reward to me, as a volunteer, is enumerable.

Amy used a broad band of photos across her layout to pay tribute to the time and energy given by a volunteer firefighter, showcasing her hero in action and at the station. The bottom section of the page provides a detailed description of the volunteers' selfless acts of heroism, which they so willingly contribute in addition to their chosen careers. A simple acrylic word charm beneath the page title sums up the main goal of any firefighter—to preserve life at all costs.

Supplies: Patterned paper (Imagination Project); textured cardstocks (Bazzill); acrylic word (KI Memories)

EYES IN THE DARKNESS OF SMOKE

In honor of her husband's heroic call to duty as a firefighter, Lana designed this page to describe a typical day-in-the-life. Pull-out journaling describes the daily routine in the station and urgent times of dismissing thoughts of danger to save the life of another. The faux charred wood patterned papers are the perfect background for this page, overlaid by the photo of her husband accented by a fire hydrant charm. The love of such a passionate job shines forth on Lana's page, as does her love for this hero.

Supplies: Patterned papers (K & Company, Karen Foster Design); letter stickers (K & Company, Karen Foster Design, Sticker Studio); mini brads, fire brigade-themed stamps, crackle stamp (Stampin' Up!); letter stencil (Home Depot); ribbon (Offray); buckle (Junkitz); fire hydrant charm (source unknown); cardstock; stamping inks; marker

EYes in the darkness of smoke

TO HIM, HE IS NOT A HERO. ITS JUST HIS CALL TO DUTY.

HERO

Henry Joseph Bisson "Chip" Temple Texas Firefighter 12-25-04

BReath in the absence of air

Lana Bisson, Killeen, Texas

TO PROTECT & SERVE

Holly created this page in honor of her father's career in law enforcement. She scanned her dad's actual police badge into her computer and combined it with a photo and title text before printing it out. A combination of patterned papers matted with black cardstocks seem to almost pop from the page, while monogram letters and two large cut-out circles soften the crisp lines and steely coolness of the layout.

Supplies: Patterned papers (Basic Grey, Junkitz); rub-on letters (Chatterbox); monogram letters (Basic Grey); label maker (Dymo); mini brads (Making Memories); cardstock

Holly VanDyne, Mansfield, Ohio
Photos: Cindy Wendling, Mansfield, Ohio

PROTECT & SERVE

April Anderton, Springville, Utah

April used enlarged and layered photos for the entire upper portion of this layout, yielding a masculine strength perfect for a police sergeant theme. She used a midnight sepia filter to soften the look of the photos for a timeless quality that reinforces the notion "once a sergeant, always a sergeant." Fingerprint accents set in opposing corners add aesthetic flair and further enhance the title.

Supplies: Image-editing software (Adobe Photoshop CS); backgrounds and brushes (www.digitalscrapbooking.com)

TOOL TIME

For an entire summer, Suzanne's husband, Mark, spent every weekend constructing his uncle's lake home. She showcases some of her favorite images of her man at work by layering them atop blue cardstock rectangles in offset fashion to coordinate with the blueprint patterned paper. Suzanne used distressed-effect, tool-themed background paper to tie the page together and added retro-illustrated sticker accents of her husband's favorite "toys."

Supplies: Patterned papers (Karen Foster Design, Sticker Studio); stickers (Sticker Studio); stitched tag (Chatterbox); hand-dyed tag (www.mytreasurequest.com); cardstock

Suzanne Makowski, Farmington Hills, Michigan

EXCELLENCE IN CRAFTSMANSHIP

Andrea Lyn Vetten-Marley, Aurora, Colorado

Admiration for her father's meticulous skills and pride in his work is evident in this tribute to excellence. Andrea used a marble-style tile as the background for her layout and framed the page, photo and journaling with strips of wood trim—both representations of the skilled work in the photos. Leather lacing used to fasten down a laminate sample tag displaying the date lends a masculine roughness and additional texture to the design.

Supplies: Textured cardstocks (Bazzill); peel-and-stick floor tile, wood trim (Lowe's); rub-on letters (Making Memories, Me & My Big Ideas); chipboard letters (Making Memories); leather lacing (Tandy Leather Company); solvent ink (Tsukineko); laminate sample

HERO

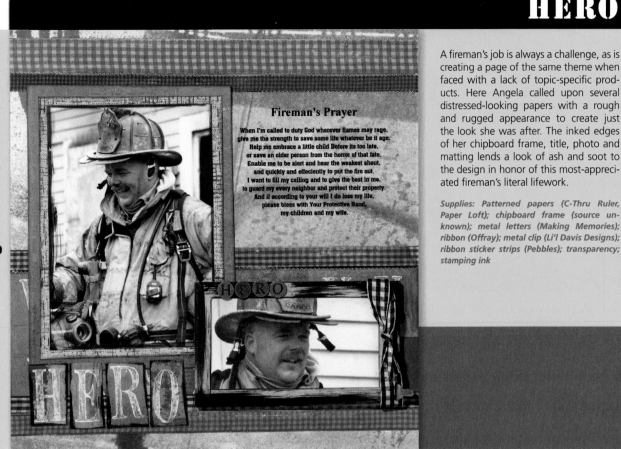

Angela Moen, Casco, Maine

Fireman's Prayer

When I'm called to duty God wherever flames may rage,
give me the strength to save some life whatever be it age.
Help me embrace a little child Before its too late,
or save an older person from the horror of that fate.
Enable me to be alert and hear the weakest shout,
and quickly and effeciently to put the fire out.
I want to fill my calling and to give the best in me,
to guard my every neighbor and protect their property.
And if according to your will I do lose my life,
please bless with Your Protective Hand,
my children and my wife.

A fireman's job is always a challenge, as is creating a page of the same theme when faced with a lack of topic-specific products. Here Angela called upon several distressed-looking papers with a rough and rugged appearance to create just the look she was after. The inked edges of her chipboard frame, title, photo and matting lends a look of ash and soot to the design in honor of this most-appreciated fireman's literal lifework.

Supplies: Patterned papers (C-Thru Ruler, Paper Loft); chipboard frame (source unknown); metal letters (Making Memories); ribbon (Offray); metal clip (Li'l Davis Designs); ribbon sticker strips (Pebbles); transparency; stamping ink

ON THE JOB

Courtney is often told how many ways she is like her father and hopes that his strong work ethic is one of those inherited traits. She created this page to focus on the ways her father showed, rather than simply told, her how to be successful in life. Courtney layered the first letter in her title to give the impression of a tire and combined it with the mailbox letters and rivet to reflect her dad's work as owner of an auto repair shop. For a fun alternative to a typical journaling block, Courtney cut her journaling into strips to allow the patterned papers to show through.

Supplies: Patterned papers (Chatterbox, Crossed Paths); letter stickers, word sticker and rivet (Chatterbox); mailbox letters (Making Memories); staples

I'm glad he's my dad: Reason #152:

He taught me the importance of a good work ethic.
My dad has been a successful businessman for many years, but none of those years have been spent behind a desk. Instead, Dad works with his hands. And he works hard. Since 1977, my Dad has been the owner of Precision Automotive, an auto repair shop in Dixon, IL. When I was little, I guess I didn't understand why my dad was always working. Now that I'm older, it really makes sense. He was working for us. He was working so we would have not only the things we needed, but also the things we wanted. More importantly, he taught me the importance of working hard, of finishing what you start, of not quitting. He didn't TELL me how to be successful; he showed me. I know in a lot of ways I'm like my dad. I've heard the phrase "Boy, you are your father's daughter" more times than I can count. I hope that includes this aspect of his personality because I can't think of a better compliment.

Courtney Walsh, Winnebago, Illinois

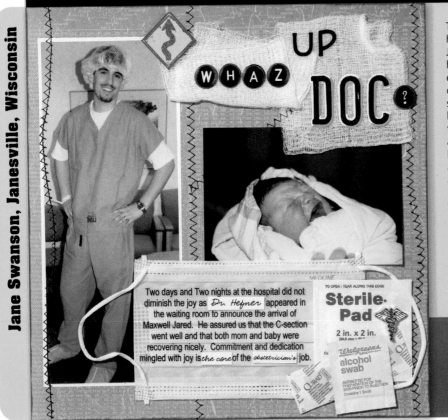

Jane Swanson, Janesville, Wisconsin

The true blue dedication found in the hearts of obstetricians shines through in Jane's tribute to the doctor who delivered her son. Rub-on stitches add visual interest while playfully capturing the theme of a successful C-section. Jane used a soft blue printed cardstock to play up both the scrubs in the focal photo and the arrival of her new baby boy. She added thematic authenticity to the page by adhering her printed transparency to a surgical mask and including actual first aid supplies as embellishments.

Supplies: Printed cardstock, arrow die cut, transparency (Club Scrap); rub-on stitches (My Mind's Eye); letter stickers (All My Memories, Sarah Bond, Sticker Studio); medical mask; sterile pad; alcohol swab; plastic adhesive bandage; gauze

Two days and Two nights at the hospital did not diminish the joy as *Dr. Hefner* appeared in the waiting room to announce the arrival of Maxwell Jared. He assured us that the C-section went well and that both mom and baby were recovering nicely. Commitment and dedication mingled with joy is *the core* of the *obstetrician's* job.

PT

Soothing patterns of blues and greens lend a calming joy to Valerie's page that celebrates her husband's new career as a physical therapist. Paper molding strips showcase her husband's new title and tie the page together with a masculine effect. Canvas phrases, photo turns and brads add additional texture and dimension to the page. For a meaningful touch, Valerie designed this layout using the same color palette and patterns she plans to use to decorate his office.

Supplies: Patterned papers, frames, molding (Chatterbox); canvas phrases (Li'l Davis Designs); index tab (7 Gypsies); letter stamps (FontWerks); date stamp (Making Memories); mini brads (American Tag Co.); photo turns (Junkitz); letter tiles (EK Success)

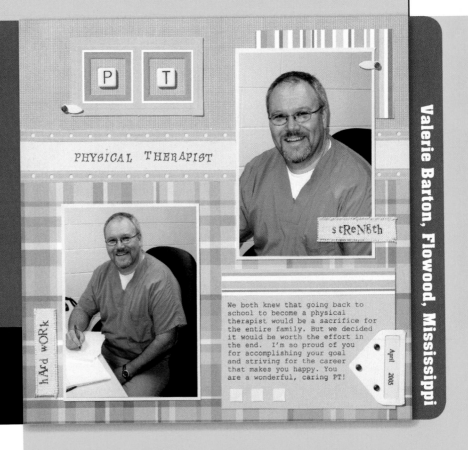

PHYSICAL THERAPIST

stReNgth

hArd wORk

We both knew that going back to school to become a physical therapist would be a sacrifice for the entire family. But we decided it would be worth the effort in the end. I'm so proud of you for accomplishing your goal and striving for the career that makes you happy. You are a wonderful, caring PT!

April 2005

Valerie Barton, Flowood, Mississippi

FINDING HIS NICHE

Kimberly wanted to give this photo of her civil engineer husband a look that truly captured his profession. She took the photo by looking over his shoulder with her digital camera in natural light, then used image-editing software to illuminate the image by changing the lighting filter to "solarization." Kimberly kept the layout simple and structured with an overall look that reflects his long-sought-after career.

Supplies: Textured cardstocks (Bazzill); letter stickers (American Crafts); photo turns, brads (Junkitz); epoxy numbers (Creative Imaginations); concho (Scrapworks); cardstock

FINDING HIS NICHE

Kimberly Kesti, Phoenix, Arizona

As a typical teenager right out of High School, Keith didn't really know what he wanted to do with his life. He signed up for Community College and finished a year of that before the lure of move to Arizona took root and off he went, lock, stock and barrel. He started off washing airplanes...in the summer... on hot tarmac. Have to give him credit for that! His other jobs were many and varied; everything from roofing and electrical work to moving furniture and woodworking.

But, a common thread emerged – Keith loves building things; putting pieces of a puzzle together to make a working whole. With this in mind, back to college he went. This time, it stuck. Civil Engineering caught, and held, his imagination. He graduated in 1993 and loves his chosen field. What guy wouldn't love building roads and bridges and tunnels? Keith sure does! As for me, I'm just grateful that you've finally found your niche. *I love you! Kim*

COMPUTERIZED ENGINEERING

From working in the yard at Arban & Carosi to overseeing large projects projects like 901 New York Avenue. You've come a long way!

Dana Swords, Doswell, Virginia

Computerized ENGINEERING inc

28 years, off and on, of working in the pre-cast industry. Your career has taken a totally different direction than you originally anticipated. You've come full circle from that job cleaning up in the yard at age 15 to Project manager.

Dana designed this page as a visual milestone of how far her husband has come in his career. Once responsible for cleaning up at a concrete production yard, he now is an engineer of the same concrete panels he helped make years ago. Cardstock arrows poised along the edge of the page give a sense of awe to the scale of the buildings he engineers and capture the feeling of distance to showcase just how far he's come. An attached business card adds a formal effect and a touch of professional pizazz.

Supplies: Patterned papers, rub-on letters (KI Memories); letter stickers (American Traditional Designs, Provo Craft, Sticker Studio); cardstock; stamping ink

The title on Kathy's layout took away the need for any additional journaling. After 42 years as a math teacher, her dad's retirement fell at just the right time for him to do many fun things with his grandchildren, rendering the ultimate equation for fun as the sum of one granddad plus two boys and two girls. Kathy chose bold dark colors to keep a masculine feel to the page and used black-and-white letter stickers for contrast.

Supplies: Patterned papers (Karen Foster Design, Scenic Route Paper Co.); rub-on letters (Making Memories); letter stickers (American Crafts, Bo-Bunny Press, Chatterbox, Mustard Moon, Sticker Studio); ribbon (Offray); large letter stencils (Plaid); monogram charm (source unknown); paint chip; playing cards; stamping ink

Kathy Fesmire, Athens, Tennessee

THE PHOTOGRAPHERS

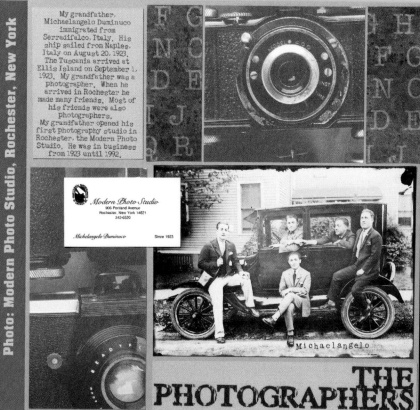

Heidi Anne Giebel, Liverpool, New York

Photo: Modern Photo Studio, Rochester, New York

My grandfather, Michaelangelo Duminuco immigrated from Serradifalco, Italy. His ship sailed from Naples, Italy on August 20, 1923. The Tuscania arrived at Ellis Island on September 1, 1923. My grandfather was a photographer. When he arrived in Rochester he made many friends. Most of his friends were also photographers. My grandfather opened his first photography studio in Rochester, the Modern Photo Studio. He was in business from 1923 until 1992.

Modern Photo Studio
906 Portland Avenue
Rochester, New York 14621
342-6520

Michelangelo Duminuco   Since 1923

Michaelangelo

Heidi's grandfather was a photographer who immigrated from Italy in 1923 and ran a photography studio in New York for almost 70 years. When she stumbled upon this photo of him with all of his photographer buddies, she knew she had to create a memorial layout that celebrated his accomplished career. Camera patterned paper provides the perfect find for her page theme, while an actual business card contributes an authentic and personal finishing touch.

Supplies: Patterned paper (Die Cuts with a View); textured cardstocks (Bazzill); letter stamps (Making Memories); distress ink (Ranger)

ART

Responsible for filling numerous roles at work such as computer technician, Web designer and customer service representative to name but a few, Mark loves it when he has the opportunity to learn about the art of glass-blowing in his "spare" time. Joanna used mica and alcohol ink to create a blown-glass effect on the page and to mimic the shape of the glasswork in the photo. For visual impact, she used white text on a black background and placed it behind a negative strip, dedicating the last negative space for the Web address of her husband's work.

Supplies: Patterned paper (Rusty Pickle); textured cardstock (Bazzill); diamond rub-ons (My Mind's Eye); rub-on letters, negative strip (Creative Imaginations); mica (USArtQuest); copper staples (Making Memories); alcohol ink (Ranger)

Joanna Bolick, Fletcher, North Carolina

Mark has many roles at work to keep him busy: computer technician, web designer, customer service rep, and operations manager. On occasion he has the opportunity to learn from Bob about the art of blowing glass, and it's always fun to see what he's created in his "spare" time. 5.1.05

Shelby Valadez, Saugus, California

HARD WORK PAYS OFF

Johnny's Job: His View
I manufacture medical equipment for arthroscopic surgery. I am a manufacturing engineer. It is my job to decide how to run products through the company in the most efficient method for cost and productivity. I design fixtures for holding parts, program CNC machines, and I also incorporate automated processes.

Johnny's Job: My View
For as long as I have known Johnny (and even before that), he has worked at Classic Wire Cut. When I met him, he was running the machines that are the backbone of CWC, the Wire EDM machines. He moved on to being supervisor of that department and is now learning engineering, something he has wanted to do for a long time. My husband is one of the smartest people I know. I don't know how the machines run, but I do know that CWC is one of the top producers of arthroscopic surgery tools, and I love hearing about what these tools are used for. I am proud of all that he has accomplished, and the fact that he has been at his job as long as he has. I am proud of his work and how dedicated he is.

DEDICATION · PRIDE · DETERMINATION

At age 15, Shelby's husband was sweeping floors as a shop boy. Now he helps design and manufacture the medical equipment for one of the top producers of arthroscopic surgery tools. In this page, Shelby expresses her admiration and pride in her husband for his dedication to hard work and perpetual learning. She used a he-said/she-said journaling approach to represent both her husband's view of his job along with her own perspective. Soft, muted tones in masculine hues give the page a clean and simple feel, while patterned paper corners and a letter stencil unify the look.

Supplies: Patterned papers (Basic Grey, Me & My Big Ideas); textured cardstock (Bazzill); chipboard letter stencil, foam letter stamps (Making Memories); watermark ink (Tsukineko); distress ink (Ranger)

TECHNICALLY SPEAKING

Purchasing their first computer years ago was a huge financial stretch for a young married couple. But Ginger's husband made a promise to make it more than pay for itself in the direction his career was heading—and boy, did it ever! Now he heads up a team of the best of the best in his field of technology, so Ginger designed this page to express her pride and the gratitude for where that first computer has led. To create a high-tech feel, she used a CD-ROM as the background for a collage of business cards, photo and name tag, overlaid with a metallic paper-punched title. She also removed the prongs from several thumbtacks and adhered them to the page.

Supplies: Textured cardstocks (Bazzill); letter punches (EK Success); label maker (Brother); solvent ink (Tsukineko); metallic paper (source unknown); thumbtacks; business card; name tag; CD-ROM

TECHNICALLY SPEAKING

IT'S MORE THAN A CAREER
IT'S A PASSION

Ginger McSwain, Cary, North Carolina

PUDDLE JUMPER

Although her husband is affectionately dubbed a "puddle jumper" by the big dogs of the airline industry, Samantha used this layout to celebrate his fulfillment of his dream of sharing the same sky with planes of all shapes and sizes. A deep maroon background gives a hefty weight to the page, balanced by chrome-enhanced stencils and shiny embellishments. To create the remainder of her title, Samantha colored canvas with a white paint pen, stamped individual letters and cut each out, mounting each word over inked and frayed canvas elements for a well-traveled feel.

Supplies: Patterned papers (American Traditional Designs, Paper Love Designs); canvas paper (Me & My Big Ideas); stencil letters (Office Depot); mesh (Magic Mesh); screw head brads (Karen Foster Design); letter stamps (La Pluma); round decorative brads (American Traditional Designs); washer words (Making Memories); chrome spray (Krylon); solvent ink (Tsukineko); pilot wings; stamping ink; pens

Samantha Walker, Battle Ground, Washington
Photos: Jonathan Walker, Battle Ground, Washington

CALLED

Courtney Walsh, Winnebago, Illinois

While landing a job at their church seemed such an easy fit for Courtney's husband, it eventually spiraled into so much more. Now an ordained minister, Courtney's husband heads up the fine arts department at their church, and this page sings the praises of his creative calling. Courtney layered festive-colored, patterned paper and die cuts with stapled ribbons for a graphic approach and added music-themed elements to play up his job title and the joy he finds within it.

Supplies: Patterned paper, die-cut circle and squares, Scripture quote (Crossed Paths); epoxy stickers, printed transparency (Creative Imaginations); ribbon (Michaels); foam letter stamps (Li'l Davis Designs); acrylic paint; gel pen; staples

SUCCEED

A new job, a new office and a new lease on life are celebrated here on Margie's computer-generated page that shares her pride in her husband's success. She used a dark striped background accented by a frame, all downloaded from the Internet to create the look of professionalism. Definition embellishments lend visual interest and reinforce the theme of success in its natural environment.

Supplies: Image-editing software (Adobe Photoshop); backgrounds, frame (www.digitalscrapbookplace.com)

Margie Lundy, Troy, Ohio

Allen is so happy in his new office, in his new role, at his new job, in this new town. He's given up a lot to provide for our family. He's worked so hard, learning, changing, growing, studying, even moving. And it all seems to have come together for this job. He is one awesome Operations Manager and Dad! 1-28-05

TECH TALK

Jennifer S. Gallacher, Savannah, Georgia

Computer terminology is merely a second language for Jennifer's husband who eats, sleeps and breathes networks, motherboards and processors in his job as a computer technician. Here Jennifer showcases select elements of her husband's foreign world with close-up images of the numerous computer parts and pieces that can be found in each and every room of their home. She juxtaposed whimsical and technical-looking patterns on the page to bring out the contrast between their two worlds in a playful way.

Supplies: Patterned papers (7 Gypsies, SEI); textured cardstocks (Bazzill); snaps (Making Memories); chipboard numbers, bottle caps, rub-on letters (Li'l Davis Designs); letter stamps (PSX Design); photo corners (Canson); eyelets; stamping ink

MAKING THE DEADLINE

making the DEADLINE

Paul's always on a deadline. He's constantly working and thinking about them, and worried that he is not going to make the due date. He has been working at Fremont Bank for a few years now, and ever since he's started, I have constantly heard the words, "I have a deadline to meet!" I worry about him working under so much stress and know when he is really busy because I call and he says he can't talk. His voice is different and he sometimes forgets to say good-bye. I know he's working on one right now because I have been hearing those 6 words again, "I have a deadline to meet!" I don"t know how he does it but he always seems to make them!!

Deadlines are the driving force behind Suzy's husband's success in his banking career. She can always tell when he's "under the gun" by the change of tone in his voice and certain telltale trademark habits. In this page, she showcased him hard at work, surrounded by stamped borders of the infamous word that keeps him forever on task. Inked edges and circles help pop the images and journaling and add a touch of playfulness.

Supplies: Patterned papers (Fancy Pants Designs); textured cardstock (Bazzill); photo turns, mini brads (Making Memories); letter stamps (Technique Tuesday); distress ink (Ranger)

LIVING THE AMERICAN DREAM

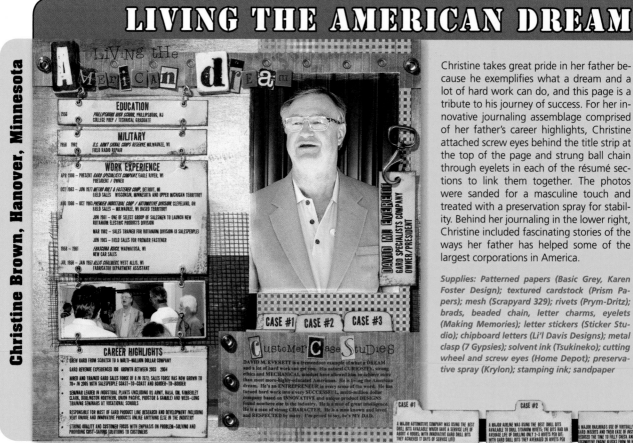

Christine Brown, Hanover, Minnesota

Christine takes great pride in her father because he exemplifies what a dream and a lot of hard work can do, and this page is a tribute to his journey of success. For her innovative journaling assemblage comprised of her father's career highlights, Christine attached screw eyes behind the title strip at the top of the page and strung ball chain through eyelets in each of the résumé sections to link them together. The photos were sanded for a masculine touch and treated with a preservation spray for stability. Behind her journaling in the lower right, Christine included fascinating stories of the ways her father has helped some of the largest corporations in America.

Supplies: Patterned papers (Basic Grey, Karen Foster Design); textured cardstock (Prism Papers); mesh (Scrapyard 329); rivets (Prym-Dritz); brads, beaded chain, letter charms, eyelets (Making Memories); letter stickers (Sticker Studio); chipboard letters (Li'l Davis Designs); metal clasp (7 Gypsies); solvent ink (Tsukineko); cutting wheel and screw eyes (Home Depot); preservative spray (Krylon); stamping ink; sandpaper

THE JOB HUNTER

Using image-editing software, Kristin created this innovative design to chronicle a grueling job search that eventually resulted in a happy ending for her family. She designed the Rolodex cards at the top of the page by scanning an actual one into her computer to use as a template. She then cut and pasted screen shots and photos of different elements of her husband's job search into a selected area inside each card template. These creative elements, in addition to a dynamic journaling box, all lead up to the face of a proud new employee.

Supplies: Patterned vellum (Chatterbox); blue staples (Target); image-editing software (Adobe Photoshop); hole punch (Marvy); corner rounder (EK Success)

Kristin Holly, Katy, Texas

THE COMMUTE

Joanna took a humorous look at her husband's typical morning, highlighting the quirky details of the start of each day. Free-falling numbers stamped along the left accentuate the notion of time chronicled in the layout. Joanna created the high-speed effect in the photo by using a slow shutter speed and setting the camera to take multiple frames. As her husband drove by, Joanna followed the car with her camera, which gave a blurred-speed effect to the background but kept the car in focus.

Supplies: Patterned paper (Chatterbox); textured cardstocks (Bazzill, Rusty Pickle); foam number stamps (Making Memories); rub-on words (C-Thru Ruler); acrylic paint

Joanna Bolick, Fletcher, North Carolina

the commute

6:30	what is that awful noise? ugh. the alarm.
6:35	get kicked out of bed by wife, who promptly steals covers and pillow and falls back asleep
6:45	eat 3 bowls of Peanut Butter Crunch as quietly as possible
6:55	pack lunch, brush teeth, and kiss slumbering wife goodbye
7:02	locate hat, coat, wallet, and keys
7:05	head out the door and wave at Cole, who is already awake and staring out his window
7:07	start up audiobook on iPod
7:08	pull away from the curb and begin another day
7:20	join everyone else on the freeway, pondering once again how many days it is until school gets out and traffic will be lighter
7:45	arrive at work
7:46	is it time to leave yet?

Hit the Road

DAILY ROUTINES

Melodee Langworthy, Rockford, Michigan

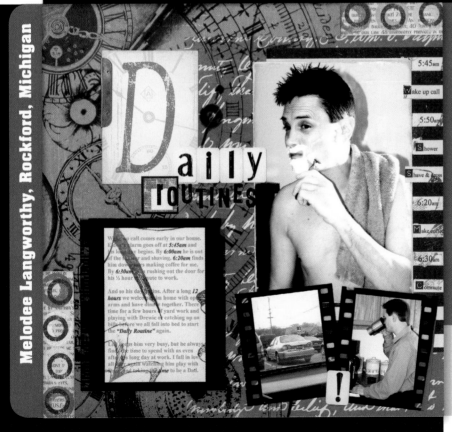

Despite a busy schedule and a jampacked day, Melodee's husband, Eldon, always finds time for his family. She created this page using a large clock-themed transparency as a backdrop and accented the page by providing a moment-by-moment account of an average morning along the right. Her journaling, set inside a negative strip, also describes the "daily routine" in their home in further detail, highlighting each time in bold. The photos perfectly illustrate each stage and express her appreciation for all he does.

Supplies: Patterned papers (Fancy Pants Designs, Scenic Route Paper Co.); letter stickers (Mustard Moon, Scenic Route Paper Co.); negative strip (Creative Imaginations); printed transparency (K & Company); metal clasp (7 Gypsies); stamping ink

U.S. SOLDIER IN THE ARMY

Inspired by the photographic timelines often found in textbooks, Holle created a visual timeline of her husband's military career, focusing on all the family support he has had throughout the years of fulfilling his dream. Since childhood, Holle's husband knew he would be a soldier, and the featured photos illustrate the journaling he typed up himself for the layout. Holle kept the page design simple by using Army colors and self-adhesive foam spacers behind her patterned paper title elements for visual interest and depth.

Supplies: Patterned paper (K & Company); cardstock

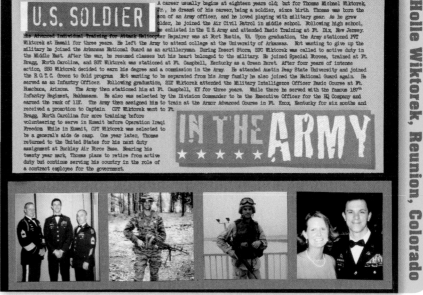

Holle Wiktorek, Reunion, Colorado

NAVY CAREER

Becky Kent, Hilliard, Ohio

Photo (submarine photo): Christian Viera, www.navy.mil

To commemorate her husband's Navy career, Becky took a photo of his uniform along with some of his medals and printed the image onto a transparency. For journaling, Becky captured the long-distance love affair she and her husband shared during those years by having her husband write his own thoughts on his career and the importance of his wife through it all. Becky included her reply "letter" and emphasized the theme of medals throughout with ribbons and military-themed nailheads.

Supplies: Patterned paper (Karen Foster Design); textured cardstock (Prism Papers); rub-on letters (Making Memories); ribbon (Michaels); decorative nailheads (K & Company); stamping ink; transparency; pen

Amy Teets, West Memphis, Arkansas

Jason in Iraq for Operation Iraqi Freedom 2003.

US MARINES

Amy's husband brought home nearly 17 rolls of film used while deployed in Iraq with Operation Iraqi Freedom. She created this digital page to highlight some of the images he will never forget during his time spent refueling and rearming military aircraft overseas. She downloaded the background from a Web site and layered it with powerful images of a job well done.

Supplies: Background from Anna Aspnes-Operation Enduring Freedom Scrapkit (www.scrapbookelements.com)

AMERICAN STRENGTH AND COURAGE IS NOT A MASK WE WEAR, OR AN OUTFIT WE DON. IT IS A STRENGTH THAT SHINES OUT FROM INSIDE. IT IS AN INNER FLAME KINDLED AND NURTURED BY THE SACRIFICES OF OUR FOREFATHERS. BURST TO BRILLIANCE BY THE THREAT TO OUR LIBERTY AND THE LOVED ONES WE HOLD DEAR. — MARINE CORPS

AN OFFICER AND A GENTLEMAN

Military pride shines forth on Tami's layout, which conveys the polished look of Navy dress whites and the admiration Tami has for her senior naval officer husband. Her journaling gives appreciation for his dedication to both his patriotic duties and his roles as husband and father. Gold photo corners finish off the look of the page with the feel of a Navy ensemble.

Supplies: Metallic paper (Paper Adventures); textured cardstock (Bazzill); photo corners (Canson)

I know it's not a very original title, but I think it really does fit you. As a senior naval officer, you are confident of yourself and your capabilities, yet you are not arrogant or brash. You look totally handsome in a dress white uniform. You give a 110% of yourself to your work and when you are home you give another 110% to the kids and me. You take your duties as husband and father as seriously as you do your duties as an officer in the Armed Forces. Did I mention how handsome you look in those dress whites?

February 2005

An Officer
&
a Gentleman

Tami Davis, Silverdale, Washington

HUMVEE

Considered luxury vehicles in America, in Afghanistan Humvees are tools of the military trade. Kelli created this page to show her military husband in action, 4-wheeling for freedom overseas. For an authentic touch, Kelli used letter stamps used by military members to label their personal gear and uniforms in order to create portions of her title. Smeared edges around the page elements create a sense of motion, as well as a tough and rugged effect.

Supplies: Patterned paper (Paper Loft); textured cardstocks (Bazzill); letter stickers (Paper Loft); Humvee die cut (Memories in Uniform); foam letter stamps (source unknown); screw top mini brads (Karen Foster Design); mini brads (American Tag Co.); solvent ink (Tsukineko); stamping inks

I guess I've known that we'd have to say our goodbye's sooner or later. It was a Sunday morning in April 2004 that you got the call from LTC Hoxey informing us it was your turn to serve our country over in Iraq. 18 months is a long time for any two people to be apart. We're both going to have to grow and take on additional responsibilities. But even more than that – we're going to have to

cultivate our relationship in unique ways to keep it as strong as it is. There are so many things that I'm going to miss about you! Having you make me laugh each day, your handy help around the house, watching you play with the boys and making new memories that would last a lifetime. I know that my heart will ache for you many times. And during those

moments, I will find comfort and strength in the faith that I have in a loving Heavenly Father who knows me personally. I am proud of your willingness to serve our country and the attitude you have carried yourself with. I pray for your safety everyday and eagerly await the day we can be united again. You are my best friend… you are my inspiration… you are my greatest love!

HUMVEES IN THE CIVILIAN WORLD (HUMMERS) ARE CONSIDERED LUXURY VEHICLES. IN RJK'S JOB THEY'RE CONSIDERED BASIC EQUIPMENT.

•AFGHANISTAN

HE DRIVES THEM THROUGH THE MUD AT HIGH RATES OF SPEED AND IT'S ALL IN A DAY'S WORK.

4 WHEELING

Kelli Lawlor, Norfolk, Virginia

FAREWELL MY LOVE

Reporting for military duty is never easy on soldiers and their families. Shandy created this touching page to honor her greatest love as he set off to protect our nation. She used an 8½ x 11" sheet of paper to create a fold-out journaling booklet to house tags featuring photos of Shandy's husband and family. She created separate tags to share what both she and their boys will miss while their hero is away. After the booklet was completed, Shandy treated the entire page addition with walnut ink for a timeless quality.

Supplies: Patterned papers (Deluxe Designs); patterned vellum (K & Company); textured cardstock (Bazzill); brads, photo turns, metal eyelet letter, jump ring, staples, paper yarn, printed ribbon (Making Memories); letter stamps (Hero Arts, PSX Design); rub-on letters (EK Success, Making Memories); leather strip (Tandy Leather Company); mini swirl clip (Creative Imaginations); label maker (Dymo); heart charm (source unknown); walnut ink (Rusty Pickle); small tag (DMD); vellum envelope; mesh; twine; letter stencil; acrylic paint

You don't need to come back a hero, you just need to come back.

Shandy Vogt, Nampa, Idaho

LIEUTENANT STEVE NOLAND USAF

Drawing from the brightly colored signs in the photograph, Barb was able to use a lot of color in her layout while maintaining a markedly masculine approach. She used an enlarged photo to comprise the bulk of the page to which she added her page title that was created using image-editing software. Barb bordered the photo with upbeat patterned paper and a simple cardstock-printed journaling block.

Supplies: Patterned paper (American Crafts); image-editing software (Adobe Photoshop); cardstock

Barb Hogan, Cincinnati, Ohio

Steve went through college at Michigan Tech on an Air Force ROTC scholarship. He was fortunate to be fresh out of college at the start of the Gulf War in 1991, and his commission was delayed until 1992. By that time, the war was over. He served his USAF time during peace time, living at both Egland AFB in Florida and Tinker AFB in Oklahoma. Given that he was an AWACS controller, he was assigned to several tours of duty in Saudi Arabia and Turkey. While at Tinker, he was one of the good Samaritans who assisted at the scene after the bombing of the Murrah Federal building in OKC. This photo was taken at Tinker AFB in Oklahoma City, Oklahoma in 1995.

THE PATRIOT

A 23-year career in the U.S. Marine Corps earned Becky's husband, Lt. Col. Christopher Fleck, this star-spangled tribute to a job well done. By using sepia-toned images and aging the elements with walnut ink, Becky gave a rugged quality and strength to her red, white and blue design. She combined several photos of her husband in action using image-editing software to create the main collage print. Texture and shine were added using fibers, a medallion accent and word pebble captions.

Supplies: Patterned papers (Doodlebug Design); textured cardstocks (Bazzill); fibers, eyelets, tags (Memory Creators); epoxy words (Li'l Davis Designs); Marine Corps medallion (K & Company); walnut ink (Ranger)

Becky Fleck, Columbus, Montana

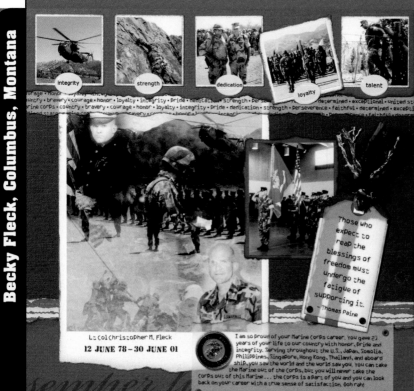

Lt Col Christopher M. Fleck
12 JUNE 78 – 30 JUNE 01

I am so proud of your Marine Corps career. You gave 23 years of your life to our country with honor, pride and integrity. Serving throughout the U.S., Japan, Somalia, Philippines, Singapore, Hong Kong, Thailand, and aboard ship, you saw the world and the world saw you. You can take the Marine out of the Corps, but you will never take the Corps out of this Marine... the Corps is a part of you and you can look back on your career with a true sense of satisfaction. Ooh rah!

2

BOYS AT HEART

Grown-up guys never outgrow fun. Just because he shaves (at least some of the time), has a closet full of suits and perhaps a mortgage to pay, it doesn't mean he's too adult to regularly indulge in man-sized helpings of pastime play. When he sets loose to shake off the stress of his every-day demands, be there to capture the kid-at-heart in action—and for photographic evidence to dispute his most outlandish fish story.

CAMPING LESSONS

Courtney Walsh, Winnebago, Illinois

The feel of the great outdoors stretches across Courtney's two-page spread that showcases a Colorado camping extravaganza. The large photo of the mountain forest is split between the two sides of the layout, setting the stage for the smaller accompanying action shots and creating a dynamic effect. For her title, Courtney affixed letter stickers to cardstock and painted white acrylic paint over them using a dry brush. She then peeled off the letter stickers to reveal the words in the paint. Courtney completed the look by painting inside the letters with a slightly darker shade of paint than the cardstock using a tiny paintbrush. Her journaling is paper-clipped inside hand-created, fold-down file folders.

Supplies: Patterned papers (Chatterbox, Me & My Big Ideas, Mustard Moon); letter stickers (Chatterbox); cardstock; paper clips; acrylic paint; gel pen; stamping ink

When **hiking**, do not pass up a campsite assuming another will appear before **dark**... chances are... **one won't**

When creating a makeshift **campsite**, try to avoid pitching your tent on the side of a hill. This makes for very uncomfortable sleeping, not to mention a huge **dogpile** of bodies in the morning.

Most importantly, do not forget to **ham** it up for the camera. No camping trip would be complete without those 'memorable' 'I'm falling off a cliff, put me on film' kind of shots!

The spirit of adventure finds a home on Lisa's two-page layout that documents an unforgettable expedition on her son William's journey to manhood. She captured an overview of this summer camping trip, selecting images that played up the weather conditions, camaraderie, work and play. Lisa achieves a rustic and raw look in her design using crumpled and distressed patterned papers, thread-torn fabric photo corners and leather accents. She also added an outdoorsy, roughing-it look by using scissors to scratch the borders which were then treated with walnut ink.

Supplies: Patterned papers (7 Gypsies, Pebbles, Sweetwater); textured cardstocks (Bazzill, Making Memories); chipboard letters (Bazzill); travel words and tags, printed twist ties (Pebbles); cardstock stickers, eyelet snaps, mini brads, leather label holders and frame, rub-on letters (Making Memories); bottle cap (Li'l Davis Designs); fabric strips (Sweetwater); distress ink, dimensional adhesive (Ranger); gel glaze pens

Lisa Schmitt, Easton, Connecticut

Photos: William Schmitt, Easton, Connecticut

VERENDRYE

EXTREME OUTDOOR

A rough-and-tumble attitude reaches new heights on Michaela's page that celebrates her husband's passion for rock climbing. She drew out the rugged rock scenery from her man in action by incorporating torn and textured papers into the design. Smudging the page edges and elements with ink pads lends further hard core effects to the page and enhances the crevices from the photos.

Supplies: Textured cardstocks (Bazzill, Creative Imaginations); woven labels (Me & My Big Ideas); letter stamps (Ma Vinci's Reliquary); die-cut letters (QuickKutz); label maker (Dymo); chalk ink (Clearsnap); stamping ink; staples

Michaela Young-Mitchell, Morenci, Arizona

extreme OUTDOOR

I taught carl to CLIMB when we first met, and we have been climbing together now for 13 years.

As carl turns 41, he is climbing HARDER than ever, pushing his LIMITs higher and steeper. Besides his physical strength, he also has the mental drive, focus, and stamina to get the results he wants. I have NO doubt this is the year he will achieve his goal to ONsight a 5.11!

(Onsight: to lead a route without prior knowledge or practice - a commendable accomplishment, indeed!)

EXTREME

PLAY HARD

OH YA!

Cheryl Manz, Paulding, Ohio
Photo and journaling: Christina Cole, Salt Lake City, Utah

RIDING the Waves

OH YA!

Play Adventure

Celebrate Life

Cheryl created this exuberant layout for her friend Christina, catching Christina's husband hard at play. The exhilarating focal photo is accentuated by layers of patterned papers and a beach-themed transparency, establishing a sensation of motion and fun. Colorful ribbons and playful accents add to the thrill-seeking page theme. Christina's own journaling on her husband's water adventure is tucked behind the main photo, while an accent photo is framed by a printed slide holder.

Supplies: Patterned papers (Creative Imaginations, KI Memories); printed transparency, slide holder (Creative Imaginations); letter stickers (Chatterbox, Sticker Studio); rub-on letters (Li'l Davis Designs); woven tag (Me & My Big Ideas); vintage tab (Melissa Frances); ribbons (Li'l Davis Designs, May Arts, Offray); spiral clip (Creative Impressions); staples; shipping tag; acrylic paint

Shuswap Lake B.C. CANADA...August 2002... what do guys do to look...as many as possible in a photograph they don't the coolest sports equipment of course! Chad had a ball wakeboarding at the cabin...gliding across the ways with perfection (pk) ok...I have to add five...

Kelli Noto, Centennial, Colorado

Cast YOUR FLY

dream BIG

there are no impossibilities

with DAD

The beauty of nature and the art of fishing combine on this masterful creation that captures a shared pastime between father and son. Kelli re-created the look and feel of her family's fishing trips in the mountains using self-adhesive foam spacers to create depth and dimension for the assorted textures featured. She created her title on separate wood veneer circles, which emerge from the fish-patterned paper like bubbles. The sanded edges of the photo exude an aged and timeless quality perfect for a page that captures a quiet moment between two of Kelli's favorite men.

Supplies: Patterned paper (Club Scrap); phrase stickers (Creative Imaginations); wood veneer; mailing label; sandpaper

We live in the suburbs surrounded by manicured lawns and asphalt streets. The days are filled with school and homework. But there are trips to the mountains that are left unstructured for time together and time to fish. Gold-Medal Waters abound near Glenwood Springs and Marble. The Roaring Fork, the Crystal, the Frying Pan, and the Colorado River teem with piscatorial delights. There are some things that you can't learn from a book and fishing is one of them. John learned to fly fish from his father and he now patiently teaches our boys. There is a science to fishing and an art. He teaches them the science of reading a hatch, picking a hole, and choosing a fly. He teaches them how to make the line dance and the art of the cast. He shares with them his time, his knowledge, and his love for the sport.

CATCH & RELEASE

Becky reveals her husband's gem of a fishing spot here on this page that flows with the essence of the great outdoors. Layers of torn papers lend an earthy undertone to the design of her husband in his element, while rustic fibers give dimension and mimic the textures of nature. A colorful, feathery grouping of fibers stretched along the bottom and wrapped around the title element further the theme of fly-fishing with the look of tied flies, while the ampersand gives the appearance of a hook.

Supplies: Patterned papers (Karen Foster Design); textured cardstocks (Bazzill); fibers (Great Balls of Fiber); decorative rivet (Chatterbox); metal ampersand, mini brads (Making Memories); stamping ink; vellum

catch & release

One of our favorite places to fish is the West Fork of the Stillwater River. Our secret fishing spot is about an hour straight up a mountain behind the mine, on a dirt road so primitive that you wonder how it got there in the first place.

Of all the places we've ever fished, the West Fork is definitely our favorite. It's a hidden treasure in the Beartooth Mountains, and because it is so difficult to get too, very few people actually fish there.

The fish are small (mostly brook trout), but they are abundant and hungry. Some of those trout will take a dry fly that's bigger than their own head! Unhooking those little buggers can be tricky, but we always catch and release, the idea being that we'll come back next year and catch them again, just a little bigger in size.

Becky Fleck, Columbus, Montana

Sheila Doherty, Couer d'Alene, Idaho

snowboarder

Snowboardin is an activity that is very popular with people who do not feel that regular skiing is lethal enough. - Dave Barry

swish

swish

swish

Most people have at least tried skiing, but not Joel, not really. He says that having your feet strapped to two different boards just doesn't make sense to him. What's to keep them from going in different directions? Snowboarding just works for him. Since he's skateboarded & surfed most of his life, snowboarding came naturally. He's pretty good at it too. He does not spend most of the time on his knees or rear end like a lot of them. And I think he looks pretty cute swishing down the mountain on his board.

January 2005

BACK SIDE

FRONT SIDE

RUSH J

LOOKOUT PASS SKI AR LIFT TICKE

The thrill of the slopes comes alive on Sheila's layout that features her snowboarding fanatic in his element. She created a sense of motion and winter rush that beckons snowboarders to play by printing action words onto the photos using her computer. Playful ephemera swoosh across the page, tied together with red ribbons and an actual ski pass. Photographs of a ski slope map provide additional authentic imagery to supplement memories from the day.

Supplies: Patterned papers (C-Thru Ruler, Pebbles); textured cardstock (Prism Papers); ribbon (Morex); metal snowflake (Making Memories); tab (KI Memories); vintage label (Cavallini Papers & Co.); round wooden letter (Li'l Davis Designs); letter stamps (PSX Design); ski lift ticket; mountain map; stamping ink

SKIING. . .

Heidi used a multitude of digital brushes to re-create the snow-blown effect of their majestic day on the slopes. Her journaling lists the defining elements of the day that her avid skier-husband chalks up to sweet perfection. The black-and-white journaling and photo block gives the page a wintry effect, while the olive and tan background at the bottom plants the page statistics in a style that is all-male.

Supplies: Image-editing software (Adobe Photoshop CS); computer brush tools: map-brush (www.vered.com); distressed brush (Rhonna Farrer); wall paper (Jenn's Sanity)

SKIING...

Cool Crisp Air

Fresh Powder

Adrenaline Rush

Incredible Views

First Tracks

Peaceful Surroundings

Catching Air

Wiping Out

Skiing the Bumps

Counting the days until next season!

DOWN HILL

bIG SkY skI ReSoRt

WINTER

SKI

**Heidi Zsupnik, Corvallis, Montana**

SNOW BOND

Debi Boring, Scotts Valley, California

Nothing brings more warmth to a wintry layout than the bond shared between father and son. Debi documented the highlights of their favorite winter pastime by filling the spread with scenes from the day. For playful dimension along the bottom of the left page, she printed two copies of each action shot and cut out the images from one of the prints. Debi set the cut-out images on self-adhesive foam spacers layered over the top of the solid photos. For journaling, she asked the special men in her life to write down their own thoughts about the day, which she then tucked and tabbed beneath the photo on the left.

Supplies: Metallic cardstock, bottle caps, date tiles (Club Scrap); printed transparency (Creative Imaginations); snowflake punches (EK Success); photo turns (7 Gypsies); label maker (Dymo); transparency; acrylic paint; brads

COLORADO-WINTER PARK

Kelli Noto, Centennial, Colorado

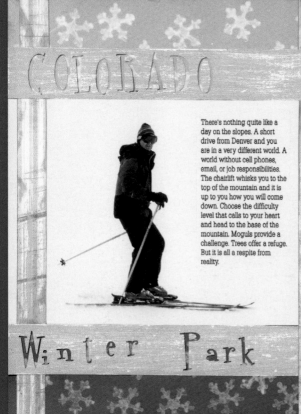

There's nothing quite like a day on the slopes. A short drive from Denver and you are in a very different world. A world without cell phones, email, or job responsibilities. The chairlift whisks you to the top of the mountain and it is up to you how you will come down. Choose the difficulty level that calls to your heart and head to the base of the mountain. Moguls provide a challenge. Trees offer a refuge. But it is all a respite from reality.

There's nothing quite like the escape that surrounds a skier on a day at the slopes. Kelli brings the quiet peacefulness found in winter-fun retreats to this page, highlighting her husband's enjoyment of a winter wonderland. She used bleach on a die-cut snowflake to create the icy effect of her background paper and framed the black-and-white photo with distressed die-cut bands of orange cardstock that give a sense of horizontal movement to the page.

Supplies: Patterned paper (Junkitz); die-cut letters and snowflake (QuicKutz); bleach; mail label; sandpaper

DRIVER'S ED

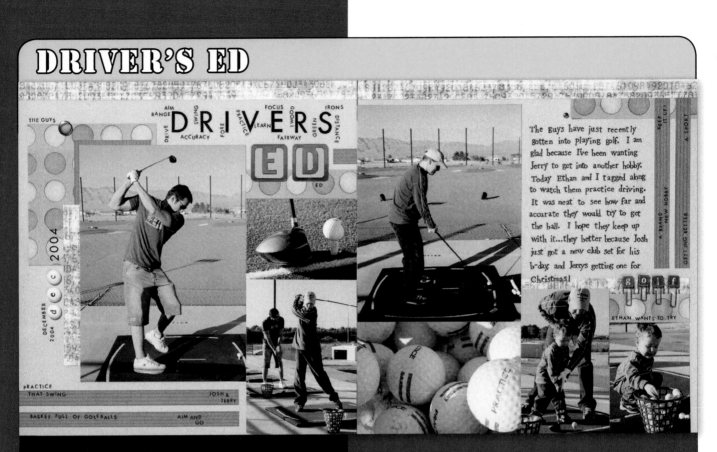

The Guys have just recently gotten into playing golf. I am glad because I've been wanting Jerry to get into another hobby. Today Ethan and I tagged along to watch them practice driving. It was neat to see how far and accurate they would try to get the ball. I hope they keep up with it...they better because Josh just got a new club set for his b-day and Jerry's getting one for Christmas!

Small rub-on letters were used on Leah's page to create thematic words in action, capturing the latest passion of all the men in her life. She was able to combine a large number of photos across her two-page spread and included several close-up shots of the balls and clubs that bond with the barrage of golf terminology rolling across the page. She repeated the shape of the golf balls throughout the spread using circular patterned papers, buttons, brads and a nailhead.

Supplies: Patterned papers (All My Memories, Creative Imaginations, Pebbles); letter clips (Jo-Ann Stores); rub-on letters (ChartPak); mini brads (Making Memories); letter stamps (Hero Arts); fabric buttons, nailhead (source unknown); cardstock

Leah LaMontagne, Las Vegas, Nevada

PASSION

Patricia's husband has been obsessed with golfing for years. In the beginning stages of this hobby, Patricia had no interest in the sport whatsoever, but after seeing what an important part of his life this pastime passion had become, she began to join him on the course. . .and now has all the more to scrapbook about his life! This page achieves a timeless feel through layers of distressed and distressed-looking patterned papers and vintage-style ephemera.

Supplies: Patterned papers (7 Gypsies, Chatterbox, Karen Foster Design, Li'l Davis Designs, Paper Loft); patterned cardstock, stickers (Club Scrap); vintage golf images (downloaded from Internet); ribbon (Scrapping With Style); rivets (Chatterbox); mini brads (Making Memories)

Patricia Jacoulot, Issy Les Moulineaux, Hauts de Seine, France

GOLF

The call of the greens provides an oasis for building friendships, much like that between Courtney's husband and father. Their common love of the game is celebrated on this sporty, masculine-themed page. Chipboard circles accented by letter stickers play well against the layout, as do a leather frame and golf charm that provide extra detail and dimension. To get the most out of her page space, Courtney has two pull-out tabs that feature extra photos and journaling.

Supplies: Patterned paper (Li'l Davis Designs); textured cardstock, chipboard circles (Bazzill); leather frame, large brads (Making Memories); letter stickers (EK Success); ribbon (May Arts); golf charm (source unknown); chalk ink (Clearsnap); corner rounder (Creative Memories)

Courtney Walsh, Winnebago, Illinois

ROAD TRIP XTREME

Diana re-created the majestic strength of the mountains her husband experienced on his "Man Trip" mountain-climbing with friends. She tore and inked mosaic-print paper and set it on foam adhesive spacers to provide a background that melds with her focal photo. Black wire mesh adds additional textural "terrain," while emphasizing the masculine look and feel. Diana accented her matted photos with wire clips attached to the metal mesh, which climb their way down the right side of the design.

Supplies: Patterned papers, bottle cap, word stickers, wire clips (Design Originals); wire mesh (AMACO); chipboard letters (Making Memories); cardstock; acrylic paint; stamping inks

Diana McMillan for Design Originals, Fort Worth, Texas

FROM CHICK CAR TO MAN CAR

Having been a good sport about driving his wife's "chick car" for several years in order to get good gas mileage, Jessie's husband couldn't wait for the day he could trade it in for something more "manly." Jessie designed this celebratory page to commemorate her husband's purchase of his much-pined-for Jeep. She kept the design fairly simple, allowing the photos to speak for themselves. Fun patterns in earthy tones give a joyful quality to the layout while maintaining a very "non-chick" approach.

Supplies: Patterned paper, word accents (KI Memories); letter stickers (EK Success); cardstock

Jessie Baldwin, Las Vegas, Nevada

MY HUSBAND'S GIRLFRIEND

A love affair with his Mustang earned Holly's husband this sleek and shiny page. Silver wire mesh melds with the grill of this metal mistress-on-wheels, while sheets of metal rev up the intensity of the layout and highlight the chrome appeal. Holly printed her journaling on a transparency and attached it to the metal journaling block with screw top snaps.

Supplies: Textured cardstock (Bazzill); metal sheets, metal mesh, rub-on letters, screw top snaps (Making Memories); letter brads (Color-bök); cardstock; transparency

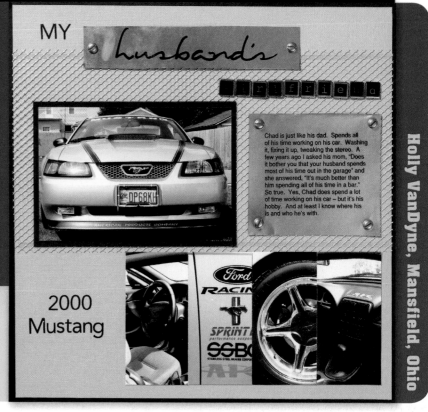

Holly VanDyne, Mansfield, Ohio

ROUGH RIDER GLENN

Samuel Cole, Stillwater, Minnesota

The thrill of off-roading excitement shines in Samuel's man-and-machine layout. A distressed and inked piece of sheet metal creates a free-wheeling background, while elements of steel and brads evoke the feel of heavy machinery. Samuel tore the background mats behind each image for the look of rugged terrain and used a graining tool to create the swirling texture. By applying black ink to the grooves and edges, he illuminated the sense of motion and added a grungy effect as well.

Supplies: Patterned paper (SEI); sheet metal, epoxy circles (EK Success); letter stickers (Words-worth); rub-on letters (Creative Imaginations); mini brads (All Sorts of Things); tags (DMD); metal photo corners (Making Memories); solvent ink (Tsukineko); alcohol inks (Jacquard Products); graining tool (Warner); cardstock; pens; stamping inks; sandpaper; fibers

CAN YOU REALLY LOVE A BIKE?

It's hot. It's cool. It's fast and sleek. Sharon designed this layout to capture the love affair the man in her life has with his bike. She plays up his need for speed by using a flowing cursive rub-on word to create a sense of motion over horizontal stripes. Sharon was able to keep the page grounded in masculinity while maintaining a theme of love by using coordinating prints with crisp, clean lines and simple shapes. She created her journaling pocket by stitching a synonym tab onto the lower right corner.

Supplies: Patterned papers (Moments Defined); metal word charm (All My Memories); letter stickers (Chatterbox); rub-on title word (C-Thru Ruler); rub-on letters (Doodlebug Design); tabs (Autumn Leaves, Melissa Frances); ribbons (Making Memories, Offray); thread, square metal clip (Making Memories); rickrack

Sharon Reynolds, Westminster, Colorado

Incredibly fast. Sleek. Powerful. You love this bike. You love the feeling of riding it. You love the looks it gets. You love me more – right?

Can you really *love* a bike

(you can!)

HARLEY

You won't catch this grandpa in a rocking chair anytime soon! Riding the open road on his Harley is where Deanna's grandpa can be found. While the overall black-and-white color scheme meshes with the photos of her grandfather's favorite toy, Deanna added a hint of Harley orange in the photo mats for added visual interest. Ball chains, license plate letter stickers, a metal label holder and black mesh all work together to establish a power-laden page with full-throttle Harley pride.

Supplies: Patterned paper, Harley Davidson sticker, button (EK Success); textured cardstocks, mini coin envelope (Bazzill); letter stickers (Sticker Studio); word charm, mini brads, silver ball chain, metal label holder, mini eyelets (Making Memories); photo turns, metal mini tabs (7 Gypsies); hemp; wire mesh; sandpaper

Deanna Hutchison, Langley, British Columbia, Canada

LIVE TO RIDE

Shaunte Wadley, Lehi, Utah

The look that coolly comes over Sam's face when he puts on his riding gear to soar the streets on his Harley has more than made up for the bike's price, according to Shaunte. Using dark rust patterned papers with vintage Harley appeal, Shaunte captures the essence of her born-to-be-wild beau. The leather eyelet trim lends the perfect effect, combining the looks of both sleek and tough, much like the bike itself.

Supplies: Patterned paper, Harley Davidson sticker, button (EK Success); textured cardstocks, mini coin envelope (Bazzill); letter stickers (Sticker Studio); word charm, mini brads, silver ball chain, metal label holder, mini eyelets (Making Memories); photo turns, metal mini tabs (7 Gypsies); hemp; wire mesh; sandpaper

MY PIANO

Samuel has played the piano nearly all his life, and the songs he creates through this passion provide the perfect outlet to express his inner voice. To create the unique look of his stamped and cropped piano accents, Samuel applied bleach to a stamp and stamped the image on black cardstock, which he then cut into three strips to assume the look of piano keys. A sheet music stamp was used to create the background paper beneath the piano key accents. To add additional finesse to his design, Samuel included a cropped photo of his hands in action that is encased by an ornate frame.

Supplies: Patterned papers (Daisy D's, Karen Foster Design); textured cardstock (Bazzill); metal square brads (EK Success); mini brads (Karen Foster Design); music charms (Darice); music score stamps (DeNami Design Rubber Stamps); piano stamp (All Night Media); metal tag, hinges, round metal-rimmed tag (Making Memories); letter stickers (Creative Imaginations); letter stamps (Hero Arts); metal label holder (Magic Scraps); round gold frame (source unknown); cardstock; chalk; stamping ink; pens; bleach

Samuel Cole, Stillwater, Minnesota

TROMBONE MAN

The blues are at their best here on Cherie's page that pays tribute to Chris' musical aptitude. She jazzes up the simple black-and-white images of the man and his brass by accenting the layout with strips of similarly toned patterned papers atop bold blocks of denim blue. For artistic edge and creative fun, she tied a band of frayed denim fabric around the entire page and embellished it with an assortment of buttons.

Supplies: Patterned papers (Basic Grey); textured cardstock (Bazzill); letter stickers (Basic Grey, Chatterbox); rub-on date (Autumn Leaves); buttons (Doodlebug Design, Magic Scraps); colored pencil; cardstock; denim fabric

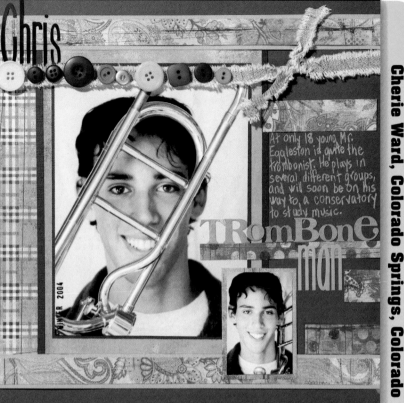

Cherie Ward, Colorado Springs, Colorado

BORDER CROSSING

Becky Thompson, Fruitland, Idaho

Becky's page sings with masculine charm, honoring the heart of musicians everywhere. She used muted, earthy tones to accompany the sepia-toned photo of these two special men in her life and their acoustic guitars. Becky created her own transparency on an inkjet printer using various fonts and favorite song titles. She played up the theme of the page by framing an actual guitar pick, which she painted a coordinating red with fingernail polish.

Supplies: Letters (Westrim); metal frame (Making Memories); guitar pick; transparency; cardstock

UNDER PRESSURE

UNDER PRESSURE

DANGER

It was Labor Day weekend 2002 and we took a drive to Indy to visit the Perry's for a nice long weekend. On Sunday, Andy and Jim took off to play golf. Nikki and I took the kids shopping then decided to come home and make a nice pot of spaghetti and meatballs for dinner since we had gone out to dinner on Saturday night.

I made the sauce as usual, but it's not always easy cooking in somebody else's kitchen. After the sauce was done, I took the pot off of the stove and set it aside to cool. Evidently, I hadn't picked the right lid for the pot because when I went to stir it, the lid seemed to be permanently attached to the pot. At first we thought that it was just hot or sticky, but we were so wrong. The sauce had "canned itself" inside the pot because the lid was too tight fitting. Nikki and I cooled the pot down, put it on ice, set it outside in the garage, and tried all sorts of things to get the pot to open to no avail. After working on it for a while, there was a tremendous

BANG

as the **LID INVERTED IN THE POT**. It scared the bejezzus out of both of us. I was also afraid that the sauce would blow up, burn my face, and make a colossal mess in Nik's all white gourmet kitchen!

After a while, the men got home and they had their own brilliant ideas and of course, they involved **FIRE**. Jim decided to **GRILL THE POT** and raise the temperature. Of course, you'd think a guy who graduated with honors in medical school would know that this method wouldn't work, but he wasn't listening to us. When setting the pot on fire didn't work, he resorted to throwing the pot against the rock pile in the back yard. After several attempts, it finally worked and the sauce spilled all over the yard. We did manage to salvage enough to eat dinner, but the real winner was Ciplo the three legged dog. Cip got to eat nearly three pounds of meatballs that night then slept for nearly 24 hours. The pot was obviously history. If Nikki lets me cook in her kitchen again, it'll be a true leap of faith.

So what IS it with guys and **FIRE?**

A red-hot memory of a Labor Day cooking mishap is fueled by detailed journaling and illustrative photos on Barb's humorous two-page spread. She used the right page to share the story of spaghetti sauce sealed in its pot and two "manly men's" solution for the situation—which involved fire, of course! The brightly colored papers create the feel of a barbecue and play on the humor of men and their seemingly primal fire "fixation."

Supplies: Patterned papers (KI Memories); letter stickers (Creative Imaginations, Wordsworth); metal-rimmed tags, mini brads (Making Memories)

Barb Hogan, Cincinnati, Ohio

MY JETTA

April 2003

my 🅥 Jetta

Wendy G. Lust, Circleville, Ohio

real car

real profession

real independence

turbo

Wendy designed this turbo-charged page to commemorate her son's landing a job in his profession prior to graduation, a feat that enabled him to buy his first set of "real" wheels. She embellished the page with silver molding, screw top brads, metal label holders and tags to enhance the hardware effect of the vehicle. Image-editing software was used to "sup-up" the smaller photos of her son in his car, playing on the power of his new and oh-so-cool first car.

Supplies: Patterned papers (Basic Grey); foam letter stamps, rub-on letters, screw top brads, metal-rimmed tags, colored staples, silver molding strip (Making Memories); metal label holders (Li'l Davis Designs); ribbon (Offray); cardstock; acrylic paint; stamping ink

HE'S NO CHICKEN

Shannon has always been in love with the childlike spirit of her husband and his daredevil tendencies. When she saw the intensity on his face and in his toes in this photo, she knew the chicken-themed paper would be the perfect fit for this page. The enlarged photo captures the heart of her man in action with transparency-printed journaling layered over the top. Shannon cut out several of the poultry images from the patterned paper and mounted them on self-adhesive foam spacers for a playful effect.

Supplies: Patterned papers (Rusty Pickle, Scenic Route Paper Co.); canvas tag, ribbons (Li'l Davis Designs); rub-on letters, letter stamps, metal dimples, antique tag (Rusty Pickle); feather charm (source unknown); jump rings (Junkitz); transparency; chalk

HE'S NO CHICKEN

Shannon Taylor, Bristol, Tennessee

One of the things I love most about my husband is his youthfulness! Sure he's finally matured into a great hubby, father & provider but he's still a kid inside! He loves to kayak, hike and road bike when he gets the chance! He loves to camp in the snow & cross country ski! And he loves to do cannonballs into the swimming pool! I love it! Most adults don't spend much time perfecting diving tricks into the pool. In fact, he may be one of the only fathers I've seen at Cedar Valley who even jumps off the diving board at all. I find myself giggling & begging for him to do it again & again! I just love the look of intensity in his face when he flies through the air! He takes such pride in his tricks! Hope he never loses this wonderful trait! Rob - 2004

IT'S OFFICIAL, EARLY EDITION UNLEASHED!

THE G.F.J. CHRONICLES AND COURIER NEWS

Glenn Johnson, spotted picking out the early edition of the Sunday paper at a local store in Stillwater, Minnesota, keeping his tradition alive. "It's my time to find out the news for the Twin Cities and for the world in general, both good and bad".

RITUAL STAYS STRONG, WEEK AFTER WEEK, YEAR AFTER YEAR

Every Saturday afternoon, Glenn Floyd Johnson, 41, makes a trip to a local convenience store to pick up the latest copy of the Sunday Pioneer Press, the St. Paul paper, early edition. He rarely misses a week, and even if he is away on vacation or on a business trip, he makes sure to read it when he gets back in town. He pours over every section of the paper, taking it all in, making sure he is aptly caught up on all the local current events, including; weather reports, business news, stocks and trading information, volunteer opportunities, classifieds, travel ideas, political columns, sports, letters to the editor, obituaries (yep, he reads through these too), store closings and sales, current movie listings, entertainment headlines, employment opportunities, and advertisements galore featuring the "best prices, guaranteed" from various stores in the twin cities and surrounding areas.

TIMELINE STRETCHES 180 MINUTES

Glenn normally spends about 3 hours going through the entire paper the first time, and his subsequent visits from then on last about an hour. Friends believe he just wants to make sure he didn't miss anything during his first reading. Here is a breakdown of the various sections of the paper and how much time he spends reading through each one of them:

LOCAL NEWS: 60 MINUTES – "This is the meat of the paper" noted Glenn one Saturday afternoon while perusing through the story of a fire in downtown Taylors Falls, MN that burnt an entire building to the ground. "Most of the time, if it's not in this section, it's probably more fluff than stuff". Can't argue with that logic.

BUSINESS & REAL ESTATE: 45 MINUTES – "This is the Who's Who and What's What part of the paper in terms of business activity. It's keep me alert of best practices in company strategies and issues that surround the corporate and nonprofit arenas," says Glenn, looking annoyed that I keep asking him questions while he is reading.

TRAVEL: 25 MINUTES – "Some of the best deals I have ever seen are located within the small print of this travel section. You just have to look intently and you'll find them" stated Glenn, rolling his eyes at me when asked where we would be going on our next vacation.

CLASSIFIEDS: 15 MINUTES – "You have to be careful" was Glenn's response when asked if he'd ever buy something from the classifieds.

SPORTS, ENTERTAINMENT, AND EVENTS CALENDAR: 10 MINUTES – "Thank goodness Sam is aware of this minutia, because that means I don't have to be" responded Glenn when asked why he spends so little time reading through these sections of the paper.

AD'S: 20 MINUTES – "There are a lot of products a person can buy if they want to" reiterated Glenn when asked what he thought about the numerous inserted ad's in the paper. He also asked, "how many more questions are you going to ask me"?

OTHER SECTIONS: 5 MINUTES – "I simply peruse through the sections that don't capture my interest, and this can change from week to week depending on the stories" says Glenn in a frustrated voice, ready to give up in his belief that my questions will cease. But finally, they have come to an end...for now.

REAL ESTATE SECTION STILL A HIT WITH GLENN

"I love to see what houses are selling for these days. It seems that some of them are just outrageous, but people still seem to buy them. I just wonder how long the housing market is going to stay strong" noted Glenn when asked what he thought of the real estate "boom" that has been so prevalent in the Twin Cities over the past few years. He continued to say, "I believe interest rates will go up on new home mortgages, but hopefully that will bring home prices down a little bit...at least I hope so. It's just seem wrong that an average 2,000 sq. ft. home is over ½ million and climbing".

BREAKDOWN OF THE SECTIONS

LOCAL NEWS
CLASSIFIEDS
TRAVEL
AD'S
BUSINESS
EVENTS
SPORTS

In the above photo, Glenn points to the increasing gas prices in the Twin Cities, saying, "I am flabbergasted that gas has risen to over $2.05 a gallon".

WOULDN'T HAVE IT ANY OTHER WAY

"Glenn's weekly ritual has become so much a part of our life, and without it, Saturdays wouldn't be the same or as much fun. I have a new ritual too; making sure Glenn gets his paper and his 180 minutes to read it cover to cover. It has become a priority" said a close source to Johnson. "Plus, while he is reading his paper, I can scrapbook without interruptions as well. To sum it up, we wouldn't have it any other way" noted the close source in closing.

Johnson, below, credits his parents for his "early edition ritualism". "Growing up, I remember watching them read the paper, cover to cover, every Sunday. I guess it just stuck with me over the years".

COMIC SECTION NEEDS REVITILIZATION

"When I was younger, I loved to read the comics, but with each passing year, they seem to be getting predictable, even dumb" noted Glenn when discussing which comics, if any, he likes to read. "I remember a comic strip called 'Stanley' that I used to enjoy reading. I haven't seen it in the paper for quite awhile. Like everything, it ran its course and was cancelled. Oh, well".

5 YEAR TRADITION IN RETROSPECT

	2000	2001	2002	2003	2004
	00%	96%	85%	80%	unknown

LOCATION OF "PAPER READER" SPACE IS FINALLY DISCLOSED BY A CLOSE SOURCE

Glenn has his favorite "paper reading" spot (right) which others have become increasingly aware not to advance upon without his approval, especially during his sacred reading time. It is located on the great room floor, giving him ample room to spread the paper out, using as much space as possible. At times the floor is so covered with paper that one cannot see the rugs or the hard wood floor underneath, making it impossible for others to utilize this space at the same time. "I need a lot of room to spread everything out" said Glenn in terms his "space issues".

LOOKING TO THE FUTURE WITH ANTICIPATION AND HOPE

"I am confident in this country; in its economy, its leadership, and its people even in the midst of war and fighting" says Glenn when asked about his feelings of the current status of the USA. "We will make it."

Samuel Cole, Stillwater, Minnesota

Every week for the past five years, Glenn has had a ritual of reading the Sunday paper cover to cover in a sacred 180-minute time frame. Samuel featured this headlining hobby in a two-page spread intentionally designed to look like a newspaper. Through heartfelt and humorous journaling, Samuel walks through this habitual pastime section by section for an in-depth look behind the scenes. Using the newspaper format kept the page design simple and required little need for embellishing.

Supplies: Circle punch (Fiskars); pens; cardstock

RC CARS

It's the thrill of redesigning RC car bodies and enhancing them to take on new terrain that fuels this miniature muscle car mechanic's creative side. Carolyn crafted this page to highlight her husband's hobby, using patterned map paper to reflect the miles and adventures these small-scale speedsters are set to undertake. She accented her molding strip border with screw nailheads that exemplify the mechanical nature of the photos. The right side features small close-up shots of each RC car in its glory.

Supplies: Patterned papers (Carolee's Creations, KI Memories); textured cardstock (Bazzill); moulding strip (Chatterbox); woven label, date stamp, chipboard letters (Making Memories); monogram letters (My Mind's Eye); wooden flower (Li'l Davis Designs); screw top nailheads (source unknown); tag; string; walnut ink; staples

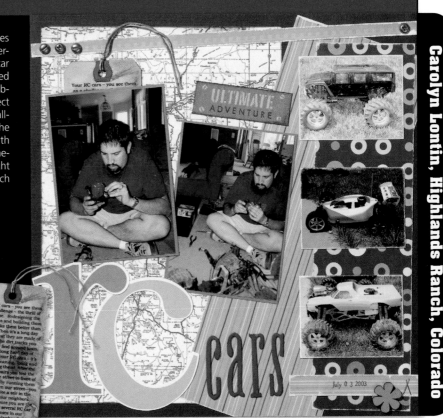

Carolyn Lontin, Highlands Ranch, Colorado

WINDSURFING

Anna Marie DeHaven, Poquoson, Virginia

The look of sheer joy and exhilaration in Anna's photo of her dear friend flows directly onto this layout. Blues and browns capture the flavor of the beach, while tiny glass marble beads give the texture of sand with shimmering pizazz. Anna placed her title quote sticker across both photo and journaling sections, uniting the overall graphic structure.

Supplies: Textured cardstocks, micro beads (Club Scrap); phrase sticker, letter sticker (Creative Imaginations); fiber (Fiber By The Yard)

If there is magic in the planet it is contained in water

Dimitrie is as passionate about windsurfing as I am about horses and scrapbooking. As with everything, he approaches his hobby with full gusto, and is a skilled windsurfer after only a few years. This day was the first time I was able to photograph him with my new 300 mm camera lens, and he didn't realize I was taking pictures at the time. The look of joy and exhilaration on his face displays his love for the sport.

Willoughby Spit
Norfolk, Virginia

May, 2003

WHITE TO BEGINNER YELLOW

Just three weeks after taking up Tae Kwon Do, Leah's husband progressed to the yellow belt. She created this page to commemorate his first milestone test in the martial art, using vibrant yellow cut-out letters to highlight the occasion. The bull's-eye patterned paper works well for imitating the progressions of colors in the Tae Kwon Do belts. Leah printed "from purity to gold ore" on yellow cardstock and set it inside the small metal frame to emphasize the symbolic meaning of the different belts.

Supplies: Patterned paper, metal frame (Scrapworks); textured cardstock (Bazzill); rub-on letters (Creative Imaginations); cardstock; ultra-fine point marker

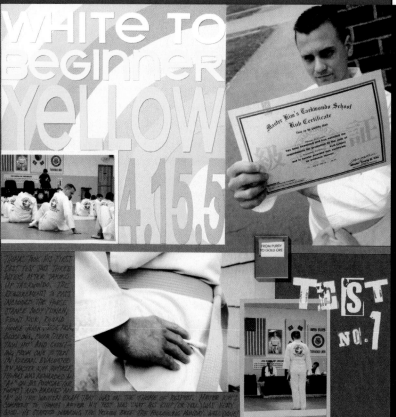

Leah Blanco Williams, Rochester, New York

PLAYING STREET BALL. . .

Jessie Baldwin, Las Vegas, Nevada

A basketball-textured paper was the perfect means for Jessie to feature the photos of her all-star street-ball player at the height of his game during a trip to Washington, D.C. She wanted to create a masculine, grungy effect to the layout to reflect the essence of the game and did so by overlapping roughed-up fonts on her computer and sanding her photo edges. Jessie set it all against a navy backdrop, pulling the design into the photos.

Supplies: Textured papers (FiberMark, Prism Papers); preservation spray (Krylon); stamping ink; sandpaper

SO CLOSE. . .

SoClose...

Barb Hogan, Cincinnati, Ohio

There has always been magic in the game of baseball. While the country watched the Boston Red Sox break the Curse of the Bambino by winning the World Series in 2004, on the small municipal fields in Cincinnati Ohio, more magic was taking place.

Kohnen and Patton has fielded a team in the Cincinnati Lawyers' League for years. While most of the other teams filled their rosters with big guys named Bubba and Hoss, K&P

filled their roster with real lawyers and bankers. Their players are men and women who spent their days working as opposed to working out, using more of their brains than their brawn. Needless to say, they never won that many games..........until 2004.

In 2004, Team K&P defied all of the odds and went undefeated in the regular season, much to their surprise and the surprise of their beefier opponents. Unfortunately, the magic of the 2004 season ended in the league

championship game when they lost by an overwhelming score. While some of their fans were quite disappointed, the players themselves will never forget their magical season.

Team photo: Keith Rabenold, Jeff Hines, Louis Schneider, Mark Combs, Dan Rogus, Roger Schoeny, Tony Caruso, Andy Hogan, Tim Rogus, Kurt Kissell. Not present: Colleen Blandford, Karen Carroll, Joe Diltz.

With more brains than brawn, this team of ordinary lawyers had a season of extraordinary success in their lawyers league—revealing the heart of true champions. Barb's two-page layout captures the intensity of the final game in which these undefeated underdogs suffered a surprising loss during their league's championship. Sanded and inked photo edges give a "plays-in-the-dirt" look to the page, while metal mesh mimics the feel of chain-link ballpark fencing. Metal frames and baseball charms effectively finish off the look.

Supplies: Patterned paper, cardstock stickers (Pebbles); mesh (Magic Mesh); frame, nailheads (Making Memories); charms (Westrim); image-editing software (Adobe Photoshop Elements); cardstock

Becky Thompson, Fruitland, Idaho

What is about football? Is it the crack of helmets and pads as players tackle each other? Is it the roar of the crowd after a touchdown? Is it the leftovers of every little boy's dream of someday being the star quarterback of an NFL team? I'm not sure, but whatever it is, this sport has Brad firmly in its grasp. Nothing gets his energy going quite like Boise State Football and his beloved Broncos, and nothing kicks off the season like the annual Blue & Orange Spring Scrimmage at Bronco Stadium. Great weather, great football - what more can one man ask for?

Blue and orange cardstocks make up the Denver Broncos-laden background on Becky's layout. Her journaling questions what it is about football that can capture the attention of her football fanatic so intently and shares his love of the annual Blue and Orange Spring Scrimmage at Bronco Stadium. To create her simple but striking design, Becky printed her journaling on cardstock and matted the photo on the journaling block. She placed a printed transparency over the focal photo and added images from the game on the right.

Supplies: Printed transparency (Daisy D's); textured cardstocks (Bazzill); photo turns, mini brads (Making Memories)

FOOTBALL FAN

Ronnie's husband was raised and groomed to be the Kansas City Chief's number one fan, and his enthusiasm for the team is contagious! Ronnie designed this layout on her computer to embrace his passion for the game and love of the team. A black-and-white image of her husband studying a football roster leads into a photo of their son who has also inherited the football fever. Textures of a football and a canvas-printed football field all lend to the theme of the page.

Ronnie McCray, St. James, Missouri

Supplies: Image-editing software (Adobe Photoshop Elements 2.0); tan canvas mat (Gina Cabrera's "For The Love of the Game" kit, www.ddecd.com); green background, leather background, football stitching, tag and metal football, metal tab label holder (Ronnie McCray, www.pagesoftheheart.net)

GO WARRIORS!

Members of the Howard household turn into Weekend Warriors from February through October, the time when rugby is under way. This enthusiastic page captures the passion Nic's husband has for his favorite team and how contagious it has become in their home. Her journaling describes the weekly preparations and accompanying emotions spurred by the big Auckland Warriors games and features a definition of the sport beneath the focal photo as well. For a look that screams with testosterone, Nic used dark, masculine colors, tough-looking fonts and metallic mesh.

Supplies: Patterned papers (Basic Grey, Daisy D's, Karen Foster Design); rub-on letters (Making Memories); mesh (from local hardware store); preservation spray (Krylon); sandpaper; stamping ink

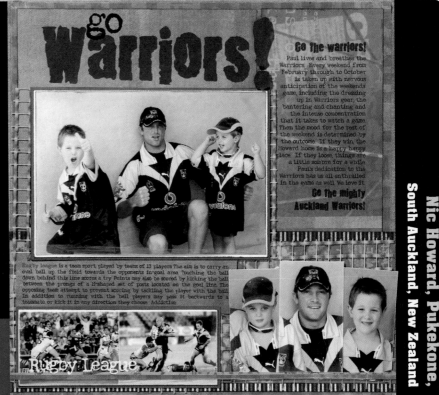

Nic Howard, Pukekone, South Auckland, New Zealand

EUROPEAN FOOTBALL

Danielle Thompson, Tucker, Georgia

Danielle gets a kick out of her husband's love of soccer (European football) and designed this page for his passion using European style. She comprised her title using various sticker and chipboard letters for an eclectic look that complements the traditional European soccer scarf sported in the photo. Danielle included black-and-white images of her champ in action, altering the backgrounds of each with an artistic filter applied in her image-editing software.

Supplies: Patterned papers (7 Gypsies, Sticker Studio); chipboard letters (Li'l Davis Designs); letter stickers (Creative Imaginations, Mustard Moon, Paper Loft, Scenic Route Paper Co.); iron-on letter (Prym-Dritz); label maker (Dymo); staples

3

FAMILY GUYS

Your man and other male members of your collective clan contribute love, laughter and happiness to the family unit in heaping proportions. Somehow the most masculine of hearts can bestow the most tender love, so be sure to capture the essence of his cherished family role and relationships with pages that prove home is where his heart is—and will always stay.

Nic Howard, Pukekone, South Auckland, New Zealand

Wanting to promote unabashed affection in their young boys, Nic and her husband, Paul, have always embraced an atmosphere of hugging in their home. Nic designed this page as a tribute to "guy hugs," comparing the standard, somewhat stifled one-armed back-slaps with the tender, full-on embraces exchanged in their family. She captured these photos at her son's birthday party as the children began doing "running hugs" into their father's arms. Chipboard letters and a bottle cap accent are all that are needed to embellish this page, as the hugs in and of themselves are a work of art.

Supplies: Patterned paper, bottle caps (Design Originals); textured cardstocks (Bazzill); chipboard letters (Li'l Davis Designs); dimensional adhesive (Duncan); stamping ink

LIKE FATHER. . .LIKE SON

Anna DiGilio, Pleasantville, New York

Anna dedicated this design to the extraordinary bond shared between her son and his dad. Distressed-looking patterned papers in masculine green and brown tones play sweetly against the black-and-white photos of Anna's son with his hero. She added acrylic paints to the filmstrip frame to blend with the patterned papers and accented the page elements with machine stitching for a crisp touch. An assortment of textural fibers and joyful word charms add dimension to the spread.

Supplies: Patterned papers (Basic Grey, Me & My Big Ideas); foam letter stamps, rub-on letters (Making Memories); eyelet snaps (Cloud 9 Design); script word laser-cut (Sarah Heidt Photo Craft); filmstrip frame (DieCuts with a View); pewter word charms (Pebbles); fibers (Fibers By The Yard); cardstock; acrylic paint

1GR8GUY

A playful, personalized license plate proclaiming Jenny's husband as "1gr8guy" has been a running joke in their relationship for years. As a second child was born into their family, Jenny was relieved to finally see the license plate retire, as it apparently wasn't compatible with a minivan. To keep the fun-filled legacy of the license plate alive, Jenny designed this page using license plate stickers, adding a tag with a photo of the plate in its prime. The focal photo lifts on hinges to share the story of this piece of the Price family history and to let her husband know that he still lives up to the infamous title.

Supplies: Patterned papers (7 Gypsies, Daisy D's, Mustard Moon); textured cardstocks (Bazzill); label stickers (Pebbles); letter stickers (Chatterbox, Sticker Studio); license plate sticker (Sticker Studio); rub-on letters, hinges, eyelets, ribbon, metal-rimmed tag, metal letter (Making Memories); woven label (Me & My Big Ideas)

Jenny Price, Farmington, Minnesota

GOING AWAY

Ginger's husband, Kent, often has to travel for his work. For each trip, he has his children fill up all his luggage with kisses so he will always be able to reach in and grab some loving affection whenever he needs it. Ginger created this page to capture the heartfelt goodbyes exchanged between Dad and family as he prepared for his longest trip yet. She used map-print vellum that features the location of "Kent" in the lower right corner and added buttons to the page for an element of homespun charm.

Supplies: Patterned vellum (K & Company); textured cardstocks (Bazzill); buttons, fabric, tag (Junkitz); stamping ink

Ginger McSwain, Cary, North Carolina

DAD

It's understandably taken years for Chris to muster up the emotional energy to create a tribute page in memory of her father, Wayne, who passed away in 1993. She divided her page into quarters, journaling what she misses most about her dad in the upper left and the questions that linger in the lower right. The other two opposing corners combine patterns of green, blue and brown tones which express the vibrancy of life her father personified.

Supplies: Patterned papers, tags and die-cut blocks (KI Memories); textured cardstocks (Bazzill); letter stickers (Doodlebug Design); distress ink (Ranger)

Chris Wasielewski, Elizabeth, Colorado

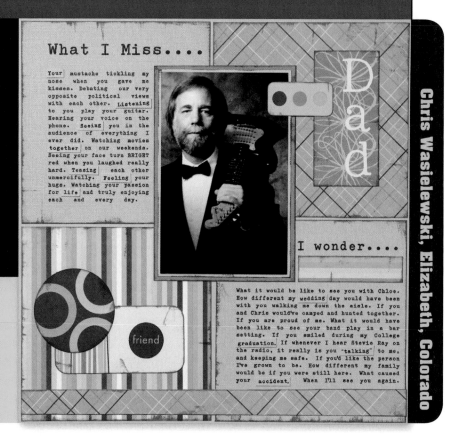

I'M SO GLAD YOU'RE MY DAD

Missy Neal, San Jose, California

After a 3-mile hike, Missy was amazed at how relaxed and happy her father looked, while she barely had the energy to snap the photo! She created this layout to cherish this fond memory of the trip the two shared. To establish a unified outdoorsy look, Missy painted along the edges of the page elements with a rich, mossy green to tie them in with the patterned paper. She stitched the blocks of patterned paper onto a black cardstock background that imitates the look of tree bark in the photos and added clay phrases and metal charms to provide a few elevated page elements.

Supplies: Patterned paper, epoxy stickers, wooden letters, metal letter charms, clay phrases, letter stickers (Li'l Davis Designs); textured cardstock (Prism Papers); foam stamp (Stamp Décor)

FATHER & SON

Samuel Cole, Stillwater, Minnesota

Although Samuel repeated the same image of himself with his father across this two-page spread, he used different-sized formats for each to create visual interest. The photo reflects the treasured relationship he shares with his dad and conveys the sincere joy they find in their bond. Samuel used tones of rust and beige combined with olive green strips, which he chalked in order to unify the page in the warmth from the photos. Decorative gold nailheads and metal label holders add texture and dimension.

Supplies: Patterned papers (Colorbök, 7 Gypsies); letter stickers (K & Company, Wordsworth); suede ampersand sticker (All My Memories); tile letters (Westrim); mini brads (Making Memories); decorative nailheads (source unknown); letter stamps (Hero Arts); metal label holders (source unknown); cardstock; chalk; stamping ink; pen

JAMES ROBERT BRADY

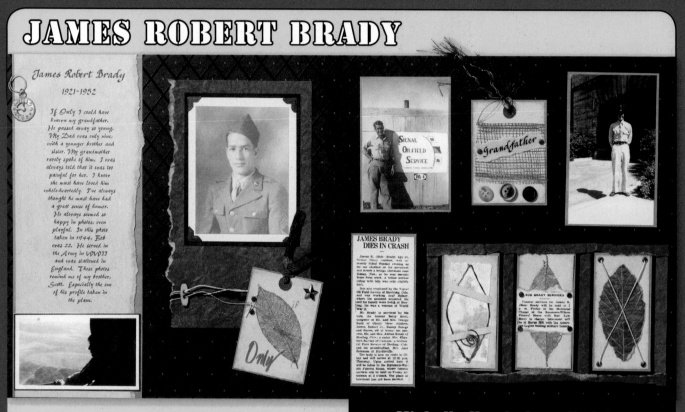

Michelle Keeth, Lowell, Arkansas

Michelle never had the opportunity to know or even meet her grandfather. But his life and his untimely death have always been a part of who she is. She designed this layout as a special memorial piece to her grandfather, sharing all she does know about him through newspaper clippings, photos and her own personal thoughts. Michelle created an elaborate, three-part frame for the right page as a holder for a memorial newspaper clipping. She repeated the skeletal leaf shape in each portion, through shaped wire and torn paper, with similar yet distinctly unique features.

Supplies: Patterned papers (Emagination Crafts, Family Traditions, K & Company); fibers (EK Success); buttons (JHB International); mini brads (Creative Impressions); photo corners (Canson); skeletal leaves (Lacey Paper Co.); star nailhead, clock charm, decorative spiral clip (source unknown); ribbon; eyelets; hemp; cardstock; wire; vellum; chalk

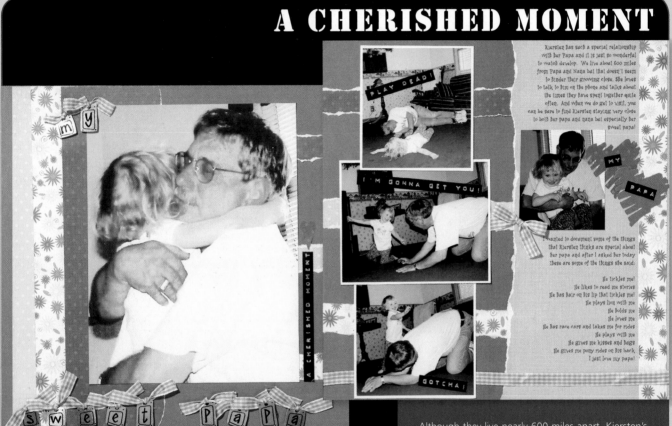

A CHERISHED MOMENT

Heather Preckel, Swannanoa, North Carolina

Although they live nearly 600 miles apart, Kiersten's relationship with her Papa is as close as can be. Heather put together this two-page spread to treasure the special bond the two share. The entire left side displays a close-up image that radiates with the love of a warm embrace. Charming metal letters, ribbons and hearts further the nostalgic, heartwarming effect. The right page features Kiersten and her Papa hard at play and journals the child's own thoughts about what makes her Papa so special.

Supplies: Patterned paper (Chatterbox); ribbon (May Arts); metal letter charms (Pixie Press); heart punch (Emagination Crafts); label maker (Dymo)

AGAPE LOVE

Inspired by the relationship between her son and his great-grandfather, Wendy created this page to showcase male bonding at its finest. Using a background of soft and subtle shades of beige and blue, she conveys a boyish charm that transcends generations. Wendy used a letter-shaped frame to accent her title word, set between black ribbons that connect with the label-maker strip at the bottom of the page.

Supplies: Patterned papers, letter frame, decorative tag (Deluxe Designs); textured cardstock (Bazzill); ribbon (Michaels); label maker (Dymo)

Agape: Love seen as spiritual and selfless and a model for humanity

Watching you and your Poppop together – playing beads, being silly with carts at the store, watching TV, playing trains, giving kisses – I have witnessed true agape love. Alex, he loves you more than you will ever know. It is truly a miracle to watch the bond between you grow. [December 2004]

Grandparents know how to do the things that warm a heart

Wendy Inman, Virginia Beach, Virginia

AMIDEI BROTHERS

Jodi's jovial page celebrates the similarities between three brothers. Rounded corners and circle-punched photos and journaling elements play perfectly against the patterned paper background. For her title, Jodi painted wooden letters with green and yellow paints and cut "brotherly" elements from a printed transparency to complete the title and also for a border element spanning the width of the page.

Supplies: Patterned paper (Li'l Davis Designs); textured cardstock (Prism Papers); printed transparency (My Mind's Eye); letters (Making Memories); circle punch (McGill); corner rounder (EK Success); acrylic paint

Jodi Amidei, Memory Makers Books

forever my brother, always my friend, forever my brother, always my friend, forever my brother, always my friend

These guys are brothers without a doubt. They enjoy each others company and all share the same silly sense of humor. The genetics are unmistakable – and the bonds run very deep.

They really are more alike than different. Sometimes it's scary how alike they can be ... right down to the way that all three of them say the wrong words to eenie, meenie, minie, mo.

Tina Freeman, Beloit, Wisconsin

always, always, always **remember**

Hugs

Your way of "Story telling"
Hearing you Laugh
Your Voice
GOING "HOME"
Going to Auctions
LATE NIGHT CONVERSATIONS
Seeing you in the garden
thankful for you
Seeing you pray
Hearing your ring tap

Hearing your boots across the kitchen floor

Shaking your FIST at me and Laughing

Whisker Rubs

MY SPECIAL memories

Dear Dad,
There are so many things I miss about you... I think of you all the time. Things I see people do remind me of you everyday. I don't even know how to begin to describe how my heart still aches with out you. I know you are no longer in pain and that you are with Jesus. That does give me little relief from the pain I live. There are so many times I want to reach out and call you and tell you this or that, and I know all I have to do is talk and you are there. You gave me that, that knowledge that belief that faith in a higher power and a better place. For that I want to thank you and for so many other things... You were such a wonderful man and the best father I could have asked for. I feel blessed to have had you and to have known you. I also feel so blessed for the time we had together and the kind of relationship we had. Thank you Daddy, I love you with all my heart.
Love
Tina

This tribute page to her recently departed father was a therapeutic means for Tina to work through the sorrow she experienced from such a difficult loss. She wrote a letter to her dad at the bottom of the page, expressing the little things she misses most about him. At the top of her page, Tina layered thoughts that remind her of him, such as his laugh and voice, using a separate font for each distinct memory.

Supplies: Patterned papers, stickers, cardstock frames, tabs (SEI); ribbons; cardstock; stamping ink

LARRY

Strips of patterned papers against a solid brown background establish a masculine look in this layout dedicated to brotherly love. Becky created her own tag to list descriptions of her brother from childhood to the present and snipped the point off the metal nailhead in order to adhere it to the tag for shine. For accents that light up the page almost as well as her brother's smile, Becky painted the letters and photo turns with a gold paint pen.

Supplies: Patterned paper (7 Gypsies, Chatterbox, Mustard Moon, Pebbles); textured cardstock (Bazzill); letters (from local dollar store); photo turns and brads (Making Memories); gold paint pen (Krylon); nailhead (from furniture supply store); cardstock; stamping ink

My brother.
The one who dreamed of soaring above the clouds.
The one who cried as a child when we broke his pencils.
The one who loves baby animals and baby children.
The one with the wicked sense of humor.
The one who can eat a pizza in a single sitting and still not gain an ounce.
The one who Adam reminds me so much of.

2-26-04

LARRY

Becky Thompson, Fruitland, Idaho

DWIGHT C. JAMES

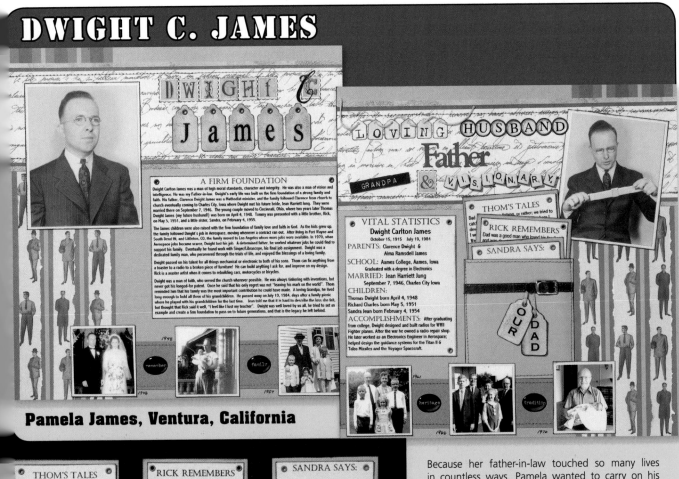

Pamela James, Ventura, California

THOM'S TALES

Dad & I used to go fishing, or rather; we tried to catch fish with little luck. I think that's where I developed my love of boats. Once, Rick, Dad, & I went fishing in Colorado, we all nearly froze! We caught one or two small trout and hung them up outside the tent. In the morning they were frozen solid. The funniest thing I remember about that camping trip was that this was one of the only times I saw Dad try to shave with a razor blade. Boy was his face a mess!

Dad was pretty busy with work, he tried pretty hard to spend time with me. Hours of talking about electronics or mechanical things gave me a great understanding of how things work. He was very good at those things. Growing up, I thought that he could fix anything. Now, my daughters think I can fix anything. Do you suppose I picked that trait up from Dad? Dad was constantly inventing things. His mechanical mind was a true gift, and I think that he found his self-worth in the things that he built and designed.

RICK REMEMBERS

Dad was a good man who loved his family and was devoted to us all. I remember a lot about him because he spent a lot of time with us and helped us all grow. In South Bend he and I would watch large airplanes fly over the house and he'd tell me what kind they were. I went with him in an old truck to a gravel pit when I was real young, where he bought a load of sand for a sandbox that he later built in the backyard. He taught me to ride a bike, and later to drive a car. His main interest was in electronics, but he was also very mechanical. I learned much of what I know from watching him repair things. He knew a lot about everything and I was very inquisitive, so it was a good match. The son of a Methodist minister, he was very religious and saw to it that we went to church ever Sunday. There were long driving trips to visit relatives in Iowa. I was always very impressed with what he did for an occupation, even though it

SANDRA SAYS:

Dad was so special to me. I was always Daddy's Little Girl. Being the youngest of three children and the only daughter, I had a very special relationship with Dad.

He was always there for me, even in the difficult teenage years, when we didn't always understand one another.

Because her father-in-law touched so many lives in countless ways, Pamela wanted to carry on his memory through this artistic celebration of his life. The old-fashioned quality of the professional vintage photos provided the perfect look for an heirloom, mixed-media style. She created a photo timeline at the bottom of the page to document milestone moments. The left page journals a history of Dwight's life and the legacy he leaves behind. The right page summarizes his statistics and displays a stitched pocket, where each of his three children share their heartfelt feelings about their father on individual tags.

Supplies: Patterned papers (Daisy D's, C-Thru Ruler, Rusty Pickle, 7 Gypsies); textured cardstocks (Bazzill); letter stickers (Club Scrap, Colorbök, Creative Imaginations, EK Success, Me & My Big Ideas, Mrs. Grossman's); epoxy letters and words, label maker sticker (K & Company); metal letters (Making Memories); dimensional adhesive (Plaid); belt buckle (Blumenthal Lansing); die-cut tags (Sizzix); Scrabble tiles; brads; eyelets; stamping inks; acrylic paint; jute; sewing machine

MY DAD

As far as Jami's family is concerned, the camera is just another appendage attached to Jami's father! Never without his camera and constantly taking pictures of every family function, Jami's dad is featured here in photos she took herself to show her appreciation for her father's hobby. She knows the photos he is perpetually taking of their family will be treasured for years to come. . .much like this page of the photographer himself. Photo corners, slide mounts and a camera charm all play up the theme quite well.

Supplies: Patterned papers (7 Gypsies); camera charm (Darice); textured cardstocks (Bazzill); decorative paper clip (EK Success); letter tags (Autumn Leaves); letter stickers (Rusty Pickle); mini brads (Making Memories); photo corners (3L); slide mounts (Loersch); playing cards; transparency; stamping ink

Jami Myers, Apache Junction, Arizona

The Photographer Of The Family

My dad is the one who always brings his camera. No matter what we are doing or where we go, he has it close by. He isn't a professional, but he takes some great photos of all of us enjoying time together as a family.
Prescott, Arizona
February 2005

DAD, YOU'RE SUCH A JOKER

Courtney Walsh, Winnebago, Illinois

My, how things have changed...

Growing up, I remember my dad as a very serious person. He worked hard all the time and had little time for entertainment. Even on the holidays, he pretty much maintained that same demeanor. Even though we knew he secretly loved the countless coffee mugs we gave him as gifts, he was never one to wear his emotions on his sleeve. Then he had grandchildren. Every year, it seems there's the arrival (or arrivals) of yet another baby... and with every one, you can see a little bit of my dad's seriousness melting away. He holds the babies, makes faces at them, talks to them in baby talk ...but he's still smart enough to give them back when they start crying.

This year at Christmas, my dad received a few notable gifts. One was a pair of black winter gloves, which, when paired with those crazy glasses made him look like the spitting image of a serial killer. In his subtle way, my dad has started to become the joker. He isn't outright funny, but he's amusing in a way that makes you think he's not doing it on purpose, as though he really wants to look like a serial killer.

I like this version of my dad. It's entertaining, soft and even a little bit sappy. He's starting to really show some of the feelings I'm sure he's had all along. I guess babies really do change people... especially tough guys. I wonder what the rest of the babies to come will do to him... we may end up with an all-out softie on our hands! But then, would that really be so bad!

All it takes is a baby to melt a serious demeanor away, as Courtney has discovered watching her hardworking father become a light-hearted grandfather. She scanned a joker card into her computer and printed it on kraft paper for a softer look that melds with the warm, woodsy tones of the page. Multimedia elements used to create the title tie in with the fibers and vintage papers that wrap up the design at the top right.

Supplies: Patterned paper, word charm (K & Company); vintage paper (Me & My Big Ideas); textured cardstock (Bazzill); snaps, spiral clip, metal letter (Making Memories); letter stamps (PSX Design); letter stickers (Colorbök, EK Success); fibers, postcard sticker, vintage stamps (EK Success); date stamp (Office Max); embroidery floss; cardstock; stamping inks; domino; hanger; corner rounder

TIME TOGETHER

Sometimes the presence of a loved one sitting nearby is all it takes for quality time. Here, Kelli features the father-and-son computer team of their household spending time together with a shared technological interest. Kelli's journaling, printed on a clear mailing label, shares her amazement of how technology has changed so drastically over the years to allow such a heartfelt high-tech moment. A band of distressed phrase stickers along the bottom unifies the page with the distressed-effect patterned paper above.

Supplies: Patterned paper (Basic Grey); phrase stickers (Pebbles); die-cut letters (QuicKutz); mailing label; stamping ink

Kelli Noto, Centennial, Colorado

NOT JUST A DADDY

Johanna wanted her daughter to get a glimpse of the man behind the daddy, so she designed this layout to accomplish just that. A file folder with the focal photo attached opens to share the clever traits and talents that make Keira's daddy such an extraordinary person, which Johanna illustrates with photos in the upper left. Johanna tucked defining labels into a slot in the lower left paper block and accented with page braces for added masculine effect.

Supplies: Patterned papers (KI Memories); file folder, rub-on letters (Autumn Leaves); letter tile (Doodlebug Design); date sticker (Creative Imaginations); letter stamps (Ma Vinci's Reliquary); ribbon (Making Memories); cardstock; page brace; sandpaper

Johanna Marquet, Mount Roskill, Auckland, New Zealand

Heather Preckel, Swannanoa, North Carolina

CONFIDANT

Secrets

Trust

Sharing

Friend

Daddy and daughter grace this design Heather created to capture their trusting bond. Distressing ink ages the page with a vintage look, lending a treasured heirloom effect to the layout. Strips of paper fastened by brads accentuate the loving features unique to Kiersten's relationship with her daddy. For a unique caption label, Heather ran a strip of paper through her label maker and inked it for emphasis and unity.

Supplies: Patterned paper, button hole stickers (Sweetwater); ribbon (May Arts); mini brads (Making Memories); staple; stamping ink; pen

BLINK

A text passage found on the Internet served as the catalyst for Julie's page, which captures the awe of a baby transformed into a young man in just the blink of an eye. Julie illustrates it perfectly by placing photos of her son as a newborn and at age 18 in between the word "blink." She adapted "Kids All Grow Up in the Blink of an Eye" by Annette Clifford to fit her layout and adhered watch parts to convey the passage of time. Inked drywall tape, clock hands and other hardware elements were incorporated to create a masculine feel, and metal items were treated with a suede paint for effect.

Supplies: Patterned papers (Carolee's Creations, Colorbök, K & Company, Li'l Davis Designs, 7 Gypsies); metal label holder, date stamp, letter stamps, mini brads (Making Memories); photo turns, watch parts (7 Gypsies); ribbon (Textured Trios); suede spray paint (Krylon); mica (USArtQuest); cardstock; watch face; clock face button; ½" conduit locknuts; drywall tape; stamping inks

BLINK

Julie McCauley, Hesperia, California

REMEMBERING A BROTHER

Ginger McSwain, Cary, North Carolina

I used to look at you, even when we were small children and think to myself what a *sweet person* you were. Such a *gentle spirit* even then, and a truly *big heart.* You were always the kind of person whose heart would break for someone else's pain and your *sweet smile* could light up a dark room. The hardest words I ever had to hear were the words that told me of your death. It has been nearly twenty years and I still mourn the loss of you in my life. You led a life that included *true friends* who loved you, a *family* that will never stop missing you and a *legacy* of *gentleness and kindness* unmatched by anyone of your young teenage years.

You are and will always be *my brother.* Your *spirit is timeless* and so is our love for you. It will go on forever. Ron's letter to the local newspaper editor after your death said it so well...for it truly WAS an *honor to know you* and be your sister...and until we see you again, we will think of you and miss you for all of our lives...my *forever brother.*

Remembering A Brother

To The Editor:
Keith Moffitt died Nov. 7, 1984, exactly two months before he was to turn 18. So many people have felt the pain and agony of the death of a loved one but if one is more as of a person who dies so young, as healthy, as suddenly. He was building his life very far. He didn't have power, money, or prestige but he had the special gifts of maturity, life and love. If you didn't like Keith, he loved you. If you didn't like Keith, he still loved you.

He was my brother and of course I'll say great things about him. Thousands of people knew him; thousands loved him. Speaking for them all, I can say only 17 but he was a great man! Despite all the disease, pain, death, and evil in this world, there is also much good — so many good people sincerely eager to help, comfort and raise the pain. Some people give flowers;

some food; some call to say they're sorry. Some people you wouldn't think care for you know they've been there and offer you anything they can. Some people offer words of hope and encouragement; some offer an ear, some a shoulder. Some people cry with you.

To the students and faculty from my nursing class; to the students and faculty at Central Davidson Senior High; to those at the American Children's Home who tipped his hat at the passing procession; to all those who cared, we say thank you so very much. The heartache is not gone and will never be totally, but I thank my God for the opportunity and privilege of being his brother and knowing him as I did. I pray that many people were blessed by his life. It was an honor to know him and until we see him again we will miss him.

Ron Moffitt
Lexington

Though Ginger's brother was merely 17 years old when he died, his family members and friends knew him as a mature and loving man. Ginger used sepia-toned photos and walnut ink throughout the page to preserve her brother's memory with timeless love and honor. She enlarged select words in her journaling and used chalk to highlight each, so that if read by themselves, a description of her brother's life is readily communicated. The central photo opens to reveal a hidden photo and poem.

Supplies: Patterned papers (Karen Foster Design, 7 Gypsies); metal hinges (Making Memories); walnut ink (7 Gypsies); chalk

We can be left with nothing greater
than gentle memories
of one who has touched
many lives in many ways.

When we gather happy memories
and hold them close to our hearts
the gentle spirit of peace
will touch us.

And as we go on celebrating
the time we had together,
we'll find the treasure
of remembering
and the comfort of believing
that such life
is indeed a gift
to be held in our hearts
forever.

Author: It Takes Two

PAPA

Amy L. Barrett-Arthur, Liberty Township, Ohio

Amy loves the relationship her youngest son and father share and designed this layout to document the special name her son came up with for his grandpa, as evidence of their unique bond. Soft fibers and suede frames enhance the tender moment captured in the photo. For a masculine yet childlike quality, Amy rolled out yellow clay tiles and aged them with a tea-stain varnish. She then stamped them with foam stamps and paint and applied the same paint along the tile borders for unity.

Supplies: Patterned paper (Chatterbox); cardstock (Bazzill); letter stamps (Hero Arts); foam letter stamps, date stamp (Making Memories); clay (Makin' Clay); canvas tags, fibers, hinges (Memory Creators); mini brads (Lasting Impressions); tea stain varnish (Rubber Stampede); acrylic paint

PA PA

Spring 2004

I am not sure where Papa came from. All the other grandkids call dad, Grandpa. But one day you started to call him Papa all on your own. Its like your own little language you have with him. You guys are pals and buddies. You get so excited when you know you are going to see him. Dad loves your name for him and Sean Nick had tried to get you to say Grandpa many, many times. You stick to your guns and continue to have your own little name for him. I hope he stays Papa to you for a long time.

Buddies   Pals

PAPA

ALWAYS NEVER SERIOUS

Although Courtney's husband and her brother have completely different personalities, they share the common trait of being perpetually hilarious. With tons of photos of the two of them being anything but serious, Courtney decided to embrace their comedic camera-shots on this playful, yet masculine page. Light-hearted patterns in dark blues and greens are given a whimsical edge with colorful, chipboard letters in the title.

Supplies: Patterned paper, textured cardstock (Chatterbox); chipboard letters (Li'l Davis Designs, Making Memories)

Courtney Walsh, Winnebago, Illinois

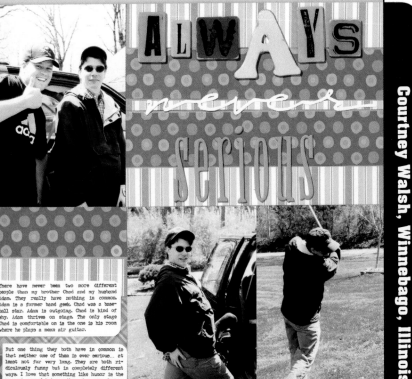

YOU ALWAYS MAKE TIME

Alecia Ackerman Grimm, Atlanta, Georgia

Photos: Deborah Ackerman, Alpharetta, Georgia

While flipping through her old baby album, the number of images of Alecia and her dad doing so many different activities together helped her pause and reflect on the generous quality time her father poured into their relationship. She played up the stripes found in her father's shirts in her background and even drew from the 1970s wallpaper to choose her word tiles. Distressing ink was used to lend a vintage quality while unifying the elements.

Supplies: Patterned paper (Rusty Pickle); textured cardstocks (Bazzill); decorative vellum, acrylic tags, acrylic words, acrylic hearts (Heidi Grace Designs); letter stickers (Mustard Moon, SEI); distress ink (Ranger); crystal lacquer (Sakura Hobby Craft); pen

EVERY BOY'S FATHER. . .

Stacie shot this image of her husband and son while they stood in line for a ride at Disney World, feeling that it captured the fascination and admiration her son has for his dad. She applied blue acrylic paint using a checkerboard stencil around the page to coordinate with her son's shirt and orange acrylic paint to create a border around the focal photo and page itself. Angling her central photo along with the title quote lent a dynamic quality to the page to help it stand apart from the busy background.

Supplies: Patterned papers (Creative Imaginations, Scenic Route Paper Co.); checkerboard stencil (Michaels); letter stickers, brads (Karen Foster Design); letter stamps (Hero Arts); painted bottle caps (Gotta Scrap!); rub-on sentiments, metal accent (K & Company); ribbons (Target); woven burlap (Gotta Mesh!); acrylic paint; stamping inks; pen

Stacie Gammill, Sulphur Springs, Texas

BE A KID AT HEART

Dana Smith, Eden Prairie, Minnesota

Dana loves the inner-child of her husband, which jumped at the chance for a spontaneous moment of fun—splashing in rainy-day puddles with his children. Playful patterned prints layered atop each other in rich, warm tones, express her husband's loving, energetic personality along with his boyish charm. The stitching and ribbons around the page add a heart-warming touch to the design, while chipboard and epoxy letter stickers provide a touch of shine.

Supplies: Patterned paper, twill (Scenic Route Paper Co.); textured cardstock (Bazzill); letter stamps (PSX Design); jump ring, photo turn (Making Memories); metal letters (K & Company); epoxy and chipboard letters (Li'l Davis Designs)

A MOMENT OF LOVE CAPTURED

Heather Keller, Humble, Texas

The special love exchanged between Heather's son and his grandpa is nestled in comfort on this warm, loving page. The layout exudes both a holiday feel and a timeless quality through the use of deep red and green patterned papers. Ribbons and twine continue the effect into the title where Heather used a multimedia assemblage that conjures the imagery of Christmas packages. Metal shine from the hinges and label holder add a hardware effect perfect for boys of all ages.

Supplies: Patterned papers (Basic Grey, 7 Gypsies); hinges, metal label holder (Making Memories); ribbon (May Arts); twine (SEI); tag (Basic Grey); rub-on letters (Autumn Leaves); slide mount; stamping ink; pen

PATH OF FATHERHOOD

Angela created this digital design to document her family's trip to Arlington Cemetery and to capture the tender moments her husband experienced with their children. She scanned an actual map of the cemetery for the background, adding texture and altering with a diamond brush. For the lettering, Angela cut out the title words from a photo taken at the cemetery. She made a copy of the letters and expanded it by 10 pixels, colored it black and layered it behind the original, accenting with a white stroke and slight bevel.

Supplies: Image-editing software (Adobe Photoshop CS, Microsoft Digital Image Pro Suite 10); background paper (www.computerscrapbook designs.com); found map

Angela Svoboda, Ord, Nebraska

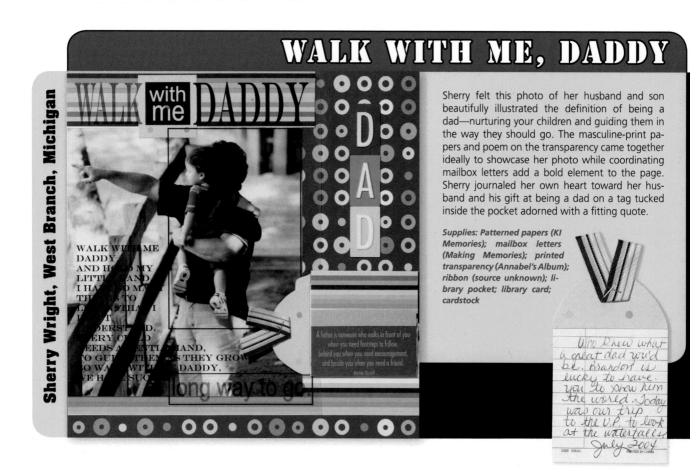

Sherry Wright, West Branch, Michigan

WALK WITH ME DADDY AND HOLD MY LITTLE HAND I HAVE SO MANY THINGS TO LEARN THAT I DON'T UNDERSTAND. EVERY CHILD NEEDS A GENTLE HAND, TO GUIDE THEM AS THEY GROW. SO WALK WITH ME DADDY, WE HAVE SUCH A long way to go.

A father is someone who walks in front of you when you need footsteps to follow, behind you when you need encouragement, and beside you when you need a friend.
Renee Duvall

Sherry felt this photo of her husband and son beautifully illustrated the definition of being a dad—nurturing your children and guiding them in the way they should go. The masculine-print papers and poem on the transparency came together ideally to showcase her photo while coordinating mailbox letters add a bold element to the page. Sherry journaled her own heart toward her husband and his gift at being a dad on a tag tucked inside the pocket adorned with a fitting quote.

Supplies: Patterned papers (KI Memories); mailbox letters (Making Memories); printed transparency (Annabel's Album); ribbon (source unknown); library pocket; library card; cardstock

Who knew what a great dad you'd be. Brandon is lucky to have you to show him the world. Today was our trip to the V.P. to look at the waterfalls. July 2004

THINGS I LOVE ABOUT BEING A DAD

Wanting to capture her husband's own thoughts and heart on a scrapbook page, Dee gave him a notebook with journaling prompts written at the top of each page so he could journal about them during free time at work. She loved the list he came up with for this particular journaling prompt and knew these photos would illustrate it perfectly. Patterned papers accented with flower punches and acrylic words give a celebratory flavor to the page while capturing the joy of being a dad.

Supplies: Patterned papers, acrylic words, rub-on lines, dots and heart (KI Memories); rub-on phrase (Creative Imaginations); rub-on date (Li'l Davis Designs); colored snaps (source unknown); thread; cardstock

Things I Love About Being a Dad

Having the responsibility of teaching my son right from wrong.

Just the sheer enjoyment of spending any amount of time with my son.

I love being a Dad to Brendan, period.

I love it when we're together, whether it's riding our scooters in the driveway, playing baseball in the yard, or just going for a ride to the store.

We both like listening to Motley Crue when we're in the truck. (How cool is that?)

Journaling October 27, 2004

Dee Gallimore-Perry, Griswold, Connecticut

October 2003

I WILL FOLLOW

Heidi created this computer-generated page during a speed scrapbooking session at an online Web site, using a magazine ad as her inspiration. She loved using the bold text against the journaling to commemorate the special bond between her father and nephew. The endearing grandpa and grandson image is enhanced by the distressed edging that melds with the photo background.

Supplies: Software (Adobe Photoshop CS); photo-editing download (Dave's Midnight Sepia); background e-paper (Ronna Penner's Shabby Shabby, www.scrapbook-elements.com)

Where ever you may go,

I will follow.

So lead on, Papa!

September, 2004
Papa has a new shadow and his name is Kaden! Kaden and Papa had a wonderful time wandering the woods behind the cabin. Kaden is all boy and helps Papa to clear out debris by picking up sticks and then throwing them down on the fort with a growl or a grunt. The point of this story is that it is always important to show those sticks who is boss!

Heidi Knight, Kyle, Texas
Photo: Kysa Hass, Owasso, Oklahoma

DAD

A straightforward, simple page design speaks volumes about the love Amanda has for her father. One large photo set beside a journaling tag exudes a pronounced strength on this layout, grounded by metal letters. The stitched cardstock and frayed ribbon soften the formality of the crisp lines, while the label holder adds a formal shine.

Supplies: Stitched cardstock (Autumn Leaves); metal letter tiles, mini brads (Making Memories); fabric (EK Success); metal label holder (Li'l Davis Designs); cardstock; acrylic paint; pen

Amanda Goodwin, Munroe Falls, Ohio

I doubt anyone loves, appreciates, or admires my dad more than I do. He is the smartest, strongest man I know. Ever since I was a little girl, I've looked up to him as he's taught me how to live by setting the best example a dad could ever set. Throughout the years, he's been my rock... always being there for whatever I need... be it a hug, a pal to join me in photography class, a loan, a dinner out, driving lessons, or any advice ranging from the topics of business to boys to God to life in general. He's my source of strength, love, wisdom, and encouragement, and he means more to me than he'll ever know.

I love you, Dad.

D A D

JUST ME AND MY DAD. . .

JUST ME AND MY DAD

WATCHING THE CARS GO BY.

two thousand and four . cate and daddy

blissful

Wendi Speciale, Cedar Park, Texas

The simple pleasure of sitting on the front porch watching the cars go by is a shared favorite pastime of Wendi's husband and son. Wendi gave the page an outdoors attitude with tranquil greens and black-and-white elements to coordinate with the photos. Ribbons stapled to the top of the page, as well as to the pull-out, pocketed photos and journaling tags, give visual excitement to this endearing father/son moment. Further whimsy is added through button "wheels" used to accentuate stamped car images.

Supplies: Patterned paper (Basic Grey); ribbon (Offray); library pocket (Autumn Leaves); vintage car rubber stamps (source unknown); solvent ink (Tsukineko); metal frame charm (source unknown); cardstock; buttons

JUST ME

MY DAD

There is nothing sweeter than watching you & your daddy on the front porch watching the cars go by. Your dad has always had a passion for

Alison Chabe, Bangor, Massachusetts
Photos: James Chabe, Bangor, Massachusetts

I stop to think of things I have never had, and it is always the first to hit me.

FaTHer

12.25.04

But is *that* why I admire him? It is nowhere close to the sole reason, but is, at this moment, the thing that especially stands out. I admire him because he is, on the most basic of basic levels, despite my constant nagging to be quieter, gentler, more rational with our children, the most perfect father. And I admire him for all of the things he is even doing--retying a toddler shoe for the thirtieth time in one day, rinsing out a long forgotten sippy cup without the gags that plague my every attempt at the same, bending with his knees to hear the tall tales of his little person's day, and because he does it with grace, and purity, and every other benevolent thing I imagined fathers were, but that util him, I could never be sure of for myself.

Photos by James

Off-centered photos taken from a child's-eye view are what make the images on Alison's page so endearing. Unaware from her own experiences of how a father should be, she now knows what it takes to be a true dad from seeing her husband lovingly interact with their children, and expresses such thoughts in her tender journaling. Alison added blocks of different textures and colors alongside both sides of her photos for a joyful feel and to repeat the shape of the photo block throughout. A tiny bow accent lends a playful touch, expressing the sensitivity that touches Alison's heart.

Supplies: Patterned papers (Diane's Daughters, Mara-Mi, NRN Designs); textured cardstock (Bazzill); cork paper (Magic Scraps); letter stickers (Provo Craft); rub-on letters (ChartPak, Creative Imaginations, KI Memories); ribbon (May Arts); wood veneer; stamping ink; pen

DEREK

As Erika's brother graduated from college, she designed this page of wisdom for him with advice for a man in the "real world." She used a simplistic design, balancing a large photo of her brother with an equal block of journaling. Erika energized the page by placing her title stickers in an eye-catching curved display. Greens and grays blend with the photo backgrounds and her brother's shirt, providing a quiet strength to the layout.

Supplies: Textured cardstocks (Bazzill); rub-on letters, definition stickers (Making Memories); letter stickers (American Crafts); cardstock

My brother Derek
Here, age twenty-three
Just graduated from college

Life. Just starting out.

My advice: **Live life.**

Make smart choices for today and tomorrow.

And don't forget to make really great memories for later.

derek

04

ESSENTIAL (ə-sen´-shəl) 1. basic; the essence of something 2. absolute necessities; indispensable

DISCOVER (di-skuv´-er) 1. to be the first to find 2. to learn of the existence of

ADVENTURE (ad-ven´-cher) 1. a daring, hazardous undertaking 2. an unusual exciting, often suspenseful experience

EXPERIENCE (ek-spir´-ē-əns) 1. act of living through an event 2. knowledge and skill gained through learning

Erika Follansbee, Goffsatown, New Hampshire

MY DAD

Diana Furey, Malvern, Ohio

Swirling patterns of various-shaped circles play up Diana's father's effervescent personality. She conveyed his love for fun on this page through layers of energetic patterned papers and brightly colored accents. By using darker tones of blues, greens and purple for the background, Diana kept the page masculine while still representing his fun-loving nature.

Supplies: Patterned paper (Imagination Project); chipboard coaster and monograms (Li'l Davis Designs); transparency

---

EVERYDAY HERO

The search for masculine embellishments was a fun adventure for Angela because she wanted to create the perfect police officer's page that reflected her husband's heroic job. She took the photo of him with their two boys in order to pause time for a moment and honor her man for his daily duty of selflessness in order to protect their community. Lined paper ripped from a notebook is bound to the page with a legal clip, creating an officer's pad for her husband to journal upon. The lower right of the page is a collage of police-themed ephemera and memorabilia, including newspaper clippings and a personalized trading card.

Supplies: Patterned paper (Karen Foster Design); textured cardstock (Bazzill); letter stickers (Li'l Davis Designs); police stickers (Creative Imaginations); buckle (7 Gypsies); twill (Making Memories); notebook paper; legal paper binder; clip; cardstock

Angela Moen, Casco, Maine

PAPA

A list of words that a father should embody is set in patterned boxes along the bottom of Prisca's heartwarming design. She placed a photo turn on the word "protector" for added emphasis, as that is the word that inspired her to create this layout around the photo of her husband and newborn babe. She used chipboard letters as a template for her title word and stitched around the page for a homespun touch. Bottle cap accents and staples add understated masculinity to the page while the soft and soothing colors encase the tender moment.

Supplies: Patterned paper (Melissa Frances, Sweetwater); letter stickers (Creative Imaginations, SEI, Sweetwater); letter stamps, number stamps (PSX Design); bottle caps (Li'l Davis Designs); woven label (from clothing in baby wear); photo turn (Making Memories); flower; staples; sewing machine

Prisca Jockovic, Morestel, France

UNCLE MIKEY

Sometimes the best family members are the ones you handpick, as Tisha describes in this page dedicated to a friend and former roommate endearingly dubbed "Uncle Mikey." Her journaling tells the story of how this special playmate, friend and uncle came to be a precious part of their family. Tisha used energetic patterns in blues and orange to evoke a childlike energy in the page and draw out the joy Uncle Mikey certainly contributes to their lives. When Tisha saw how his personality and love of her children came through in these photos, she simply knew this page had to be made.

Supplies: Patterned paper, tags (Basic Grey); letter stickers (Pebbles); rub-on phrases (Chatterbox); mini brads (Making Memories); ribbon

Tisha McCuiston, Midlothian, Virginia

4

NOT YOUR AVERAGE JOES

Some men are simply one in a million, and you take great pride in the fact that the men in your life represent more than a few of them. You've been fortunate to know and love diamonds in the rough, knights in shining armor, prince charmings and all-round extraordinary men. Some serious star treatment is called for to commemorate the guys you admire with pages that profess your appreciation—once the initial embarrassment is over, he'll thank you for it.

Michelle Keeth, Lowell, Arkansas

Michelle captured the heart of her husband (or maybe it was he who captured hers. . .) here on this earthy layout. She layered rust and black cardstocks with faux-textured and textured papers, inking and tearing select edges for effect. Netting, jute and fibers lend an adventurous feel to the page along with button relics and a frame.

Supplies: Patterned papers (EK Success, Paper Loft); netting (Jest Charming); ampersand stamp (River City Rubber Works); antique uppercase letter stamps (PSX Design); decorative mini frame (K & Company); metal label holder, mini brads, metal plaque, hinges, jump rings, photo turns (Making Memories); painted "journey" charm, wooden letters, buttons (source unknown); cardstock; stamping ink; transparency; pen; marker; acrylic paint; jute

& ENDS WITH YOU

THANKFUL

Upon seeing this photo of her husband, Derrick, Mary was overwhelmed with gratitude for the sheer realization such an amazing man is part of her life. To respect his shyness toward sentimental emotions, she hid her journaling behind the photo on a pullout tab. Mary created the patterned text paper herself, using Microsoft WordArt to type and alter the word "thankful" by playing with size and color saturation in the different repetitions. The design was kept simple, using autumn colors and stitching to capture the heart of the day. Orange-yellow floss is laced through corner eyelets, framing the photo with a down-to-earth beauty.

Supplies: Patterned paper (Scenic Route Paper Co.); textured cardstock (Bazzill); button, photo hanger, ribbon (Findings and Things); woven labels (Me & My Big Ideas); primitive heart punch (EK Success); label maker (Dymo); decoupage medium (Plaid); corner rounder (Creative Memories); eyelets; embroidery floss; stamping ink

Can we ever truly explain the love we feel for another person? Probably not. But I can try. I can stumble through it, with heartfelt, but inadequate words I can tell you that my life has led me to this point, to you. And I am thankful.

I can see your patience, your kindness, your sensitivity. All in this one photo. Maybe because I was there. Maybe because we shared that moment. Or maybe just because I love you.

You are everything to me, and when I look at this photograph I see you. Really, truly see you. And I am so glad that I find you and that you found me.

I am thankful that we found each other.

Thankful Hearts

DERRICK
SEPTEMBER.2004

EVERYTHING

A love letter to her Mr. Right takes center stage on Becky's simple yet sincere design. The white journaling block against the stark black background lends dynamic contrast to the page and illuminates the photo of the man of Becky's dreams. Pewter accents around the layout lend the same depth, strength and beauty that are found at the heart of this man. A printed transparency grounds the design over her flowing title.

Supplies: Textured cardstocks (Bazzill); metal photo corners, metal plaque (Making Memories); transparency

Brad,

Who else but you could ever be my greatest love? You - who've been there through it all - you who've stood by me when nobody else would - you who've loved me in spite of me. You who've made me laugh, made me cry, made me appreciate the finer and the sillier things of life all at once. All of the things that I truly love in my life, I've got because of you. Three beautiful, gorgeous children - a life I really do love, a relationship that I know will span the test of time - not to mention more love and support than I ever deserve. You give me reason to be the best I can - to keep trying when I just want to give up. How can I ever say thank you enough?

I look at our life these last 14 years, and I know there have been so many times when you could have walked away from it all - decided it just wasn't worth the struggle. But you never did. You are the most amazing person I've ever met. I am so blessed and grateful that you see everything in me, and love me anyway. Thank you for the last 14 years, and I can't wait to see what the next 14 are like. I love you more than you'll ever know, and not nearly as much as I know you deserve. I'll spend eternity trying to prove that you, my darling, truly are my greatest love.

My everything.

I love you.
July 30, 2004

Where there is
love
there is life

Everything

Becky Thompson, Fruitland, Idaho

THE LUCKY ONE

Beth Petry, Big Stone Gap, Virginia

And the greatest of these is love

The Lucky One

You try to tell me that you're the Lucky One...but I know, it's me. You've brought so much into my world...love, adventure, devotion, humor, desire. I could create an endless list of what you've added to my life. Your love is reckless, peaceful, confusing, and simplistic, and I cherish every ounce of it. You say you're the lucky one, but I know if the cards are all on the table I've won this hand.

In the game of luck and love, Beth feels that she has won at both. The lock and key and king and queen playing cards help to express that she and her man create the perfect pair. Beth crumpled sections of black cardstock to create a leatherlike effect then used actual leather threading to stitch around the page for a touch of testosterone. For her journaling, Beth treated a paper bag with a spray to make it acid-free, ran it through the printer, crumpled it, inked it and rolled it like a scroll.

Supplies: Patterned paper, quote (Daisy D's); metallic mesh (Magenta); antique metal key and lock (Li'l Davis Designs); card stickers (EK Success); compass stamp (Stampabilities, Craft's Etc.); letter stamps (Wordsworth); walnut ink (Foofala); metallic rub-ons (Craft-T); brown paper bag; leather lacing; stamping inks

THE COLORS OF YOU

Using image-editing software, Amber chose a specific color for each image of her beloved and coordinated it with her journaling to reveal the significance of each hue in his personality. She wet the white journaling cardstock, rolled it, ironed it and painted the edges. To distress her title, Amber dry brushed white acrylic paint over the top section, then painted the metal title letters and sanded them, coating each with clear nail polish. Brilliantly colored fabric borders add additional color and dimension.

Supplies: Textured cardstock (Bazzill); ribbon (Offray); mesh (Gotta Mesh); metal letters, brads (Making Memories); image-editing software (ArcSoft PhotoStudio); chalk; acrylic paint; clear nail polish; transparency; sandpaper; cardstock

Amber Baley, Waupun, Wisconsin

FOREVER LOVE

Maria Burke, Steinbach, Manitoba, Canada

After five years of marriage, I can honestly say that I am more in love with you today than I have ever been. It's pretty amazing how my love for you just keeps on growing. On the day we got married I thought, this is it, I love you so much things just can't get better than this. But ... somehow each day my love for you just gets fuller and more intense. Being parents has taken our marriage to the next level. Instead of losing the romance or putting our relationship to the side, I feel like we are closer than we've ever been. Seeing how much you love Sarah and want to protect her and be there for her just adds a whole new dimension to our relationship. How could I not fall head over heals in love with you every single day when I see what an amazing father you are to our daughter.

Phil, you are so thoughtful and caring. Your first concern is always to make sure that Sarah and I are happy and doing good. There is no one on this earth that I feel more comfortable with and no one with whom I can completely be myself around other than you. You are truly my partner, in absolutely every sense of the word, and there is no one else that I would rather journey through this world with.

You are the love of my life.

A love that keeps on growing is happily expressed on Maria's page dedicated to her soul mate, Phil. Her large journaling block shares a tender reflection of the journey their relationship has led them on and the ways their love has filled her heart. Carefully chosen love-themed stickers accent the photo, while two square mini brads in the lower corners add a masculine flair that draws back to the black-and-white photo.

Supplies: Patterned paper (American Crafts, KI Memories, 7 Gypsies); definition word stickers (Pebbles); letter sticker (Pixie Press); epoxy sticker (Creative Imaginations); mini square brads (Making Memories); date stamp

YOU HAVE ALL THE ELEMENTS

Maria Gallardo-Williams, Cary, North Carolina

Maria's husband is a chemical engineer and she is a chemist—it only seemed fitting for Maria to create her patterned paper by scanning and editing an old periodic table! The dimensional letter stickers place the play-on-words title front and center. She furthered the theme by using a photo of her husband in his element—woodworking in their garage. The metallic brads and textured metal label holder all add to the effect of his shop.

Supplies: Patterned papers (Basic Grey, Pebbles, self-made); letter stickers (Basic Grey, Making Memories); metal label holder (Club Scrap); shaped and mini brads (Making Memories); cardstock; stamping ink

PRIORITY MALE

Inspiration to highlight her top-priority male struck while Nancy was standing in line at the post office. She picked up a couple of Priority Mail envelopes and then it was off to her computer. Nancy scanned the envelope and eliminated most of the background using image-editing software. She then changed "mail" to "male" and printed the title in grayscale, placed it on a light table and traced the letters and logo. Nancy then scanned them back into the computer, enlarged and printed in reverse onto glossy paper then finally cut them out by hand. Her journaling is inside the stamp book reproduction, using her husband's name and age for the stamp price.

Supplies: Glossy paper (Royal Brites); metal expression charms (All My Memories); colored brads (Making Memories); stamp (Stampinks Unlimited); cardstock; stamping ink

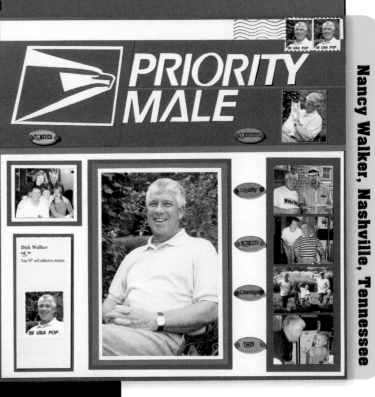

Nancy Walker, Nashville, Tennessee

8 RANDOM FACTS ABOUT HIM

Kim Mauch, Portland, Oregon

Eight random

C FACTS

He has crooked pinkies.

All animals & old people love him.

He frequently gets road rage!

He can be very sarcastic.

He won't admit that he likes cheese.

He enjoys pulling pranks on naive people.

He's addicted to Starbucks Lattes.

He can play the piano.

ABOUT him

Christian Heinz Mauch

Filled with little-known facts about her husband, this computer-generated page was created as a complement to an all-about-me page Kim had made on herself. She staggered journaling strips that feature the often-hidden information about Christian and placed a diagonal strip behind the body of the piece, creating movement and a balance of strength and visual energy throughout the page.

Supplies: Image-editing software (Adobe Photoshop Elements 2.0); papers, elements (Tonya Todd-Krassen, www.playonelements.com)

TRUE LOVE

Inspired by the beautiful persona her husband embodies, Shannon created this layout to pay tribute to the journey of their relationship, which culminated in their wonderful family and storybook romance. The leather strips with button accents capture the look of the railroad tracks in the layout with the same rugged feel displayed in the photo. Shannon's journaling block shares the tale of two crazy kids still in love after 14 years and two children.

Supplies: Patterned paper (Carolee's Creations); buttons (Junkitz); cork paper bottle cap (Anima Designs); heart stamp (source unknown); mini brads (Doodlebug Design); letter stamps (PSX Design); leather strips (Rusty Pickle)

TRUE Love

true love

It amazes me that we found each other so young. Can you believe it's been fourteen years since our first date? I often think back on that first day you came over with your strange hippy clothes and long, curly hair. We talked for so long about everything under the sun. Once you left, Mom said she wasn't so sure about you. I told her not to worry. It wasn't like I was going to marry you. Famous last words! And now, here we are with an almost 8 year marriage and two beautiful sons. Like most couples we have our ups and downs but we are always able to work through them because of our communication skills. You are such a beautiful person inside and out. I can't imagine my life without you! What I love most about you is your superiority as a father. I couldn't have picked a better man for the job! I also love to photograph you. I just wish you would be more comfortable in front of the camera and let it capture the wonderful you that I know.

Shannon Taylor, Bristol, Tennessee

I AM SAM

Samuel discovered the peaceful, happy and content feelings experienced while vacationing also reflected his attitude in life. He used the large photo from his trip to represent who he is as a person and accented the page with definition stickers that describe his personality. The shaker tag at the bottom unties to reveal his journaling and a bonus photo inside. Samuel showcased his name on the right by repeatedly stamping each letter on individual circle punches.

Supplies: Patterned papers (Chatterbox, Daisy D's, Creative Imaginations, K & Company); shaker tag (DMD); handwriting stamp (Hampton Arts Stamps); uppercase letter stamps (Hero Arts); epoxy corners, ribbon, paper reinforcements, circle punch (EK Success); photo turns (K & Company); definition stickers (Pebbles); word stickers (Karen Foster Design); letter stickers (Sticker Studio); watermark ink, solvent ink (Tsukineko); corner rounder (Creative Memories); cardstock; twine; buttons

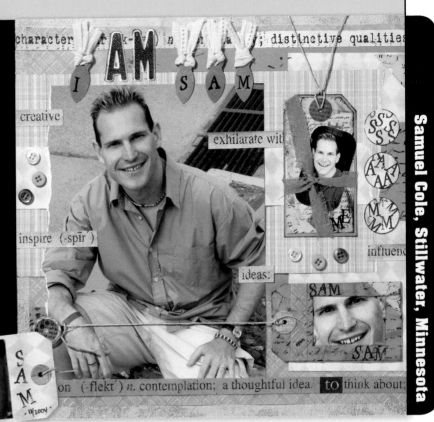

For as long as I can remember, I was under the assumption that one should not "showcase" themselves, but rather let others do it. I agree, somewhat, but who better to describe you ... than you! So I will! I am fun, kind, thoughtful, creative, witty, playful, smart & cute! I AM SAM!!

— 11/2004

Samuel Cole, Stillwater, Minnesota

MISTER HAPPY

Amy Goldstein, Kent Lakes, New York

mister happy

Everyone knows someone who always has a smile on their face and a bounce in their step, right? Well, I was lucky enough to marry one!

You always seem to be able to look at the positive side of any situation regardless of how dismal or dark it may be. You always have a kind word to say to anyone you meet. You have an uncanny way of looking at things and somehow finding the good in anything. You wake up in the morning ready to go and greet the day with a smile even before that first cup of coffee.

These are the reasons, that I am proud to say that I am married to ...

Mister Happy!!!

Amy's husband not only sees the brighter side of any and every situation, he can share his optimism and perpetual joy with those around him as well. Therefore, she made this page to express her own joy and happiness for marrying "Mr. Happy." Purple borders on the top and bottom of the page give the layout a masculine strength, infused with the complementary color scheme that play up Amy's husband's vibrant demeanor. A Mr. Happy badge adds a lighthearted element to the design and coordinates with the energetic, polka-dot patterns.

Supplies: Patterned papers, twill (Scenic Route Paper Co.); textured cardstock (Bazzill); conchos (Scrapworks); mini brads (Junkitz)

GOD'S MEASURE OF A MAN

Cindy used Scriptures that document the Biblical measures of a man to describe how her own man of God is perceived. An inked ruler accenting the border of her husband's photo adds to the theme an element of whimsy. Cindy printed the photo onto cardstock which she distressed by inking the edges. She inked the leather patterned paper as well, accentuating the grooves and textures. Cowboy charms lend the final touch to this page of adoration.

Supplies: Patterned paper (K & Company); leather paper (Paper Loft); rub-on letters, letter stamps (Making Memories); letter stickers (EK Success, K & Company); metal cowboy hat and boots charms (source unknown); cardstock; measuring tape; acrylic paint; stamping ink

Cindy Lee Sparks, North Platte, Nebraska

JOE'S FAVORITES

During a photography class, Briana captured this contemplative pose of her husband and decided to feature it alongside a list of some of his favorite things. Briana made sure to include the date at the bottom of the page in order to be able to look back in future years to see if his list remains the same over time. The distressed-looking patterned papers continue the reflective feel of the photo, using quiet, subdued colors.

Supplies: Patterned papers, tags, letter stickers (Pebbles); definition block (Foofala)

Briana Fisher, Milford, Michigan

Molly Bridges, Pelham, Alabama

Molly crafted this encouraging layout to boost the confidence of her husband and to keep him pressing ever forward toward his dreams. The bright, upbeat colors create a masculine feel through the blue and brown accents, but also conjure hopeful optimism and energy as well. Molly filled the page with printed quotes from a patterned paper series and used them to further emphasize her journaling. A single initial page pebble in the middle of the layout unites the design with a touch of shine.

Supplies: Patterned paper, quotes (KI Memories); textured cardstock (Bazzill); letter pebble (K & Company); rub-on letters (Autumn Leaves); pen

---

THE MAN OF MY DREAMS

Character counts in Stephanie's book, and she designed this page to highlight her husband's amazing personality and the defining traits she holds dear. She used her title to launch into the journaling block where label-maker labels showcase each quality Stephanie admires, which she elaborates upon through stamping. Simple layers of brown papers over a blue background set a masculine tone that is further enhanced through inked edges and smudges throughout.

Supplies: Patterned paper (Sweetwater); textured cardstock (Bazzill); letter stamps (Hero Arts); letter stickers, twill tape sticker (Pebbles); label maker (Dymo); cardstock; stamping ink

Stephanie Allbaugh, Appleton, Wisconsin

WHEN MY MAN LOVES HIS WOMAN

Suzy Plantamura, Laguna Niguel, California

For better or worse, Suzy's husband has and will always stay by her side, and this page was made as a dedication to his commitment to their marriage. She printed the focal photo on cotton twill and just slightly frayed the edges for a barely scuffed effect. Wanting to capture the heart of her husband's personality, Suzy included the range of his playful and loving personality through photos and journaling featured in the attached booklet. This page addition, combined with black stickers, photo corners and a printed tag holder, adds weight to the page, keeping a loving overtone while adding distinguished masculinity.

Supplies: Patterned papers (7 Gypsies, Daisy D's, Outdoors & More Scrapbook Decor); photo fabric (Blumenthal Lansing); decorative square stickers, letter frames, chipboard saying (Li'l Davis Designs); letter stickers (Li'l Davis Designs, Sticker Studio); love envelope, booklet, photo corners (Creative Imaginations); leather frame (source unknown); ribbon; stamping ink

LOVE XOXO

Wanting to express her deeply passionate love for her husband while keeping a masculine look to the page, Briana designed this heartfelt creation using black, white and red papers and accents. The black-and-white photo gives a classy, suave tone to the page that is accentuated by torn and rolled patterned paper. Briana added a collage-effect to the page with an assortment of sticker strips exuding all-guy appeal, proving a love-inspired layout can still look manly.

Supplies: Patterned paper (Chatterbox); rub-on letters (Making Memories); letter stickers (Pebbles); fibers (Fibers By The Yard, www.scrapbookfabric .com); concho (Scrapworks)

Briana Fisher, Milford, Michigan

JULY 3, 1993

Heather Preckel, Swannanoa, North Carolina

Heather celebrates her wedding anniversary on this design dedicated to her amazing husband. The black-and-white patterned background paper mimics the staggered look of the bricks from the wall in the photo, while the distressed-effect, red paper lends a rugged wash of rich color to the simple page. Heather used twill printed with the months of the year to highlight their anniversary month with a hand-cut heart and incorporated the month into her dated label.

Supplies: Patterned paper (Sweetwater, 7 Gypsies); twill, printed rubber band (7 Gypsies); label maker (Dymo); stamping ink

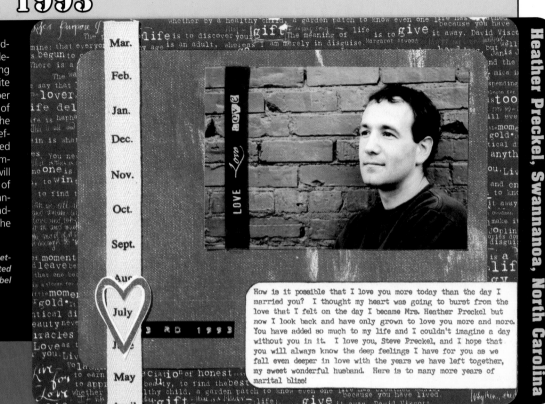

How is it possible that I love you more today than the day I married you? I thought my heart was going to burst from the love that I felt on the day I became Mrs. Heather Preckel but now I look back and have only grown to love you more and more. You have added so much to my life and I couldn't imagine a day without you in it. I love you, Steve Preckel, and I hope that you will always know the deep feelings I have for you as we fall even deeper in love with the years we have left together, my sweet wonderful husband. Here is to many more years of marital bliss!

YOUR EYES TELL THE STORY

Dana Smith, Eden Prairie, Minnesota

For Dana, the love story written between two hearts is exchanged with just one glance into her husband's eyes. She created this layout to express her deep love for such an amazing husband, father, son, friend and overall individual. The black and white color scheme accented with red conveys a formal, romantic feel that when combined with metal mesh, lends an eye-catching, masculine flair.

Supplies: Patterned papers (Carolee's Creations, Chatterbox); textured cardstock (Bazzill); letter stickers (Chatterbox, EK Success); rub-on letters, rivet, molding, frame (Chatterbox); metal word charm (All My Memories); staples, metal mesh (Making Memories); epoxy word (K & Company); ribbon (Making Memories, Offray); cardstock; stamping ink

A DENIM HEART. . .

His daily run in the rat race when he would much rather enjoy less-traveled paths earned Carrie's husband this denim-heart page. In appreciation for the dedication he has for providing for his family, this layout reflects her husband's no-nonsense style. Machine stitching lends heart-warming comfort to the page, providing decorative borders for the different elements. An overalls snap is used to open the photo-laden door, revealing the journaling of a grateful wife.

Supplies: Patterned papers, paint chips (Chatterbox); textured cardstock (Bazzill); ribbon (May Arts); denim patch (Joy Co.); stamps (Leave Memories); word and letter tiles (Card Connection); photo corners (Darice); mini brads (Boxer Scrapbook Productions); label maker (Dymo); hinges (Lowe's); solvent ink (Tsukineko); silver snap (found)

Carrie Zohn, Monroe, North Carolina

A **DENIM HEART** IN A POLYESTER WORLD. 0305

JUSTE POUR TE DIRE

Karine Cazenave-Tapie, Nieul, France

Karine created a festive, masculine layout to celebrate her husband's 28th birthday. Using playful prints in blues, greens and browns, she sets the perfect tone for her page and then brings the party to life through an assortment of colorful letter stickers and metal accents. She used an aluminum sheet to make a tag for a portion of her title and to highlight the birthday boy's special date. Journaling pulls out from a tag filed neatly inside the patterned folder on the left.

Supplies: Patterned papers (Doodlebug Design, KI Memories, SEI); letter stickers (American Crafts, Doodlebug Design, Mustard Moon, Paper Loft, Sticker Studio); vintage tabs (Melissa Frances); decorative brads (ScrapGoods, SEI); ribbons (Li'l Davis Designs, May Arts); metal letter accent (Making Memories); photo turn (7 Gypsies); solvent ink (Tsukineko); cardstock; aluminum sheet; stamping ink; chalk

juste pour te DIRE

Mika 28

ET ESCHAILER

JOYEUX UN

ANNIVERSAIRE

juste pour te dire qu'à J-2 je n'ai toujours pas trouvé ton cadeau d'anniversaire, mais tu comprends bien qu'il s'agit d'un exercice extrêmement périlleux pour moi encore une fois! Explique-moi

THE MOST SIMPLE MAN I KNOW

Holly Corbett, Central, South Carolina

the most **simple** man I know

The quote running the stretch of the right side of this layout is the life philosophy Holly's husband has embraced for years. Content with the meaningful, basic necessities in life—love, health and the fulfillment of goals—Holly created this page to capture her husband's simplistic, peaceful and most admirable take on life. A wire mesh panel behind her photos adds a rugged touch to the page which Holly embellished with paint, a few cross-stitches and a handful of buttons. Heartfelt journaling resides behind the focal photo.

Supplies: Patterned paper, cardstocks, buttons, stencil letters (Chatterbox); metal mesh (Making Memories); letter stamps (PSX Design); tab (Autumn Leaves); die-cut letters (QuickKutz); embroidery floss; stamping ink; acrylic paint

---

CRAZY MAN

Stephanie's husband especially likes acting goofy, which means she rarely if ever captures him in a somewhat serious mode. However, it's this comedic aspect of his personality that Stephanie loves most about him. Therefore, she brought out his silly side with cheery colors and playful prints on this lighthearted layout. Inspired by a layout challenge to make her own argyle pattern, Stephanie used this page to incorporate a variety of masculine patterns and textures. Flower accents embellished with clear button centers add whimsy to the page and illustrate his reigning title as "Crazy Man."

Supplies: Patterned papers (Chatterbox); textured cardstock (Bazzill); paper flowers, chipboard letters (Making Memories); clear buttons (7 Gypsies); ribbons (Chatterbox, Offray); letter stamps (Stampin' Up!); stamping ink; staples; safety pins; denim

Stephanie Johnson, Belmont, New Hampshire

D

This man makes his children scream with laughter.

This man holds my hand while we're walking.

This man fixes almost anything.

This man puts his family first.

This man two-steps and jitterbugs.

This man teaches me to change.

This man likes his food spicy.

This man gives us endless love.

You're the man.

As her husband turned 40, Rebecca created this 8 x 8" two-page layout for him to commemorate the milestone event. She kept the page design simple, keeping the focus on the photos. To create the initial on the left, Rebecca traced a chipboard letter onto cardstock and cut it out by hand. A slender journaling strip on the far right shares sincere snippets about Dave's personality, allowing the photos to illustrate.

Supplies: *Patterned paper (Basic Grey); chipboard letter (Making Memories); cardstock; craft knife*

Rebecca Bollman, Poolesville, Maryland

I LOVE YOU ANYWAY

Judith Mara, Lancaster, Massachusetts

From his unique sense of style to his laundry-sorting quirks, Judith takes a humorous look at "10 tiny little weird things" about her husband. Designed as a Valentine's Day page, the photo opens up like a card to reveal the top 10 idiosyncrasies she has come to know and love about her beau. She heat embossed the heart in the lower right corner and inked its edges for greater impact.

Supplies: Patterned paper (Li'l Davis Designs, Me & My Big Ideas); textured cardstock (Bazzill); letter stickers (Memories Complete, Mustard Moon); floral-embossed print stamp (Plaid); letter stamps (Hero Arts, PSX Design); foam letter stamps, metal letter (Making Memories); ribbon (Daisy D's, Great Balls Of Fiber, May Arts, Offray); twill (Creative Impressions); twine (SEI); acrylic paint; stamping ink

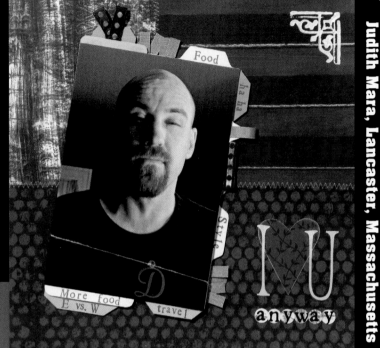

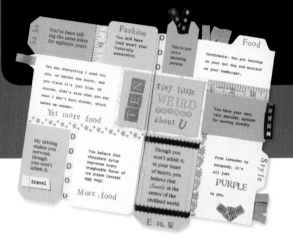

ANDY AT 26

Christie Wildes, Gainesville, Florida

Christie highlighted her husband's "arrival" at age 26 by creating this page to document just how far he's come. She painted two letter stencils to feature his age, using both outside and inside portions. The ribbons and decorative brads lend a military flair to the page, which is one of his many milestones documented in the bulleted journaling. Distressed edges around the photo and inked edges around the page contribute to the boyish charm that Andy exudes.

Supplies: Patterned paper (Deluxe Designs); textured cardstocks (Bazzill); ribbon (May Arts); decorative brads, stencils, numbers (Making Memories); letter stickers (Me & My Big Ideas); solvent ink (Tsukineko); acrylic paint

DERRICK

Mary created this page to reaffirm her husband's generous heart and selfless spirit. She kept the design simple with a no-nonsense approach utilizing dark masculine tones and patterns. She distressed the edges of the main photo with paint to blend with the worn-and-torn effect of the patterned paper title block. Eyelets set in black paper strips exude a decidedly manly and industrial look. The focal photo opens to reveal additional photos and journaling that expresses Mary's gratitude for the man she feels fortunate to have married.

Supplies: Patterned paper (Paper Loft); eyelets, hinges, photo corner (Making Memories); office stencils (Headline); cardstock; acrylic paint

DERRICK, YOU ARE A MAN WHOSE CHEERFULNESS IS UNMATCHED. EVERYDAY IS A NEW EXPERIENCE, AN EXPLORATION OF HUMAN NATURE AND A CHANCE TO HELP OTHERS. GENEROSITY COMES SECOND NATURE TO YOU, AND YOU ARE NOT AFRAID TO GO WITHOUT SO THAT SOMEONE ELSE MAY HAVE. YOUR KINDNESS DEFINES WHO YOU ARE. YOU ARE NOT A PERSON WHO LIVES FOR HIMSELF, YOU LIVE FOR OTHERS.

YOU GIVE BLOOD SO THAT OTHERS MAY LIVE, YOU HELP FAMILY, NEIGHBORS, AND FRIENDS, YOU SPONSOR THREE CHILDREN IN UNDERPRIVILEGED NATIONS, YOU DONATE YOUR TIME TO THE CHURCH, YOU GIVE MONEY TO THE MUSTARD SEED SO THAT OTHERS MAY ALSO ENJOY A THANKSGIVING DINNER. YOU TOUCH SO MANY LIVES...YOU ARE HOPE AND LIGHT; YOU ARE AN EXAMPLE OF WHAT WE ALL COULD BE.

THE SOUL THAT PERPETUALLY OVERFLOWS WITH KINDNESS AND SYMPATHY WILL ALWAYS BE CHEERFUL.

- PARKE GODWIN

Mary MacAskill, Calgary, Alberta, Canada

MY GUY

An arrangement of simple cardstock word stickers is all that was needed to perfectly express the definition of Michelle's "guy." She set bold rub-on letters and letter tags above the photo, leading into the playful complexity of patterns and words on the right. Michelle established her color scheme by the single orange stripe on her main man's shirt and repeated it in a ribbon stripe at the bottom of the image, held in place by photo turns.

Supplies: Patterned papers (Scenic Route Paper Co.); textured cardstock, ribbon (Bazzill); rub-on letters, photo turns, colored brads (Making Memories); word stickers (Design Originals); letter stickers (source unknown); jute

Michelle Tardie, Richmond, Virginia

ALEXANDER

Glenni Light, Plymouth, Massachusetts

My eyes see you in this photo as a man...
But my heart sees you...
As a newborn gazing about with big blue eyes.
As an infant belly laughing at yourself in the mirror.
As a toddler splashing in puddles!!!!
As a preschooler waving thru the school bus window.
As a school age boy reading out loud.
As a teen playing your guitar.
I never imagined the time would go by sooo darn fast!
Granted we had days that seemed eternal and I would have gladly sold you to the traveling circus.
But this photo! Oh, it makes me catch my breath and wonder...
When did I blink my eyes?
How did 20 years pass so quickly?
The one thing that my eyes and heart both see is that same great charming smile!
Live your life joyfully!!!
love mom
2/06

As her son was dashing out the door to head back to college, Glenni snapped this close-up of a nearly grown man and had to catch her breath. Her journaling recounts the ways her heart still sees her "baby boy," even as her eyes register the unmistakable image of a man. She stapled strips of the patterned paper around the black-and-white photo as a frame, giving a subtle hint of color.

Supplies: Patterned paper (Basic Grey); letter stamps (Technique Tuesday); rub-on numbers (Li'l Davis Designs); staples (Making Memories); solvent ink (Tsukineko); transparency

THE APPLE OF MY EYE

This highly original layout is the creative result of Mary's husband's patience as he worked with her to capture the perfect shots. Despite numerous camera, backdrop and prop adjustments, never once did Mary's true love tire with frustration. She altered the image with image-editing software, de-saturating the photo with the exception of the apple. Mary highlighted "apple" in her title by first printing the other words on a transparency. She then spelled out "apple" with letter stickers and painted over them, removing the stickers once the paint was dry.

Supplies: Patterned papers (DieCuts with a View); textured cardstock (Bazzill); letter stickers (EK Success); eyelets; embossing powder; acrylic paint; transparency

Mary MacAskill, Alberta, Canada

AFTER GOD'S OWN HEART

Nely Fok, El Cajon, California

faith (fāth) n. firm belief;
unwavering trust in honesty.

believe

character

dis·cover   reflection

I remember the first time I saw you worship. We were juniors in high school. Best friends. You invited me to Hope Chapel's worship night the day after thanksgiving. I didn't really know what to expect but I went with you, anyway. That night, I saw how you don't just sing words; you praise God with your voice, with music! You raised your voice and your hands, as if you were in surrender. You seemed enraptured in God's presence as you sang love songs unto Him. Having grown up in a conservative Catholic church, this was all new to me. I felt a little awkward. I didn't know if I could worship like that -- with no inhibitions -- but I admired you for doing so.

Twelve years later, you continue to amaze me with the way you worship. As we went through some uncertain times this year, there were moments when I, once again, felt unsure if I could totally surrender to God. Of course, part of me wanted to. But there was a part of me that hesitated because I didn't want Him to take what little I felt I had left. But you, you still steadfastly prayed, "Lord, all we have is yours. Take it and make it your own." Your faith and your utter surrender to God floors me. Your actions encourage me. Without preaching to me, you teach me so much. You teach me that surrender means freedom. You teach me that God truly does know the plans He has for our lives. You teach me that God is good and sovereign, and He loves me unconditionally. I thank God for the gift He's given me in you. I feel so blessed to have you for my husband— a man who truly seeks after God's own heart.

hope (hōp) n. [OE hopa] 1 a feeling that what is wanted will happen, accompanied by expectation 2 the object of this 3 a person or thing which one bases some hope - vt. hoped, hop'ing to want and expect

hope

The faith of Nely's husband has always inspired her and kept her strong, even through the trials of life. She created this layout to express how much she admires and appreciates his steadfastness. The black-and-white photos capture the essence of a true worshipper, praising God with every ounce of his being. The black and brown color scheme accentuates the photos and gives a raw and natural feel to the spread.

Supplies: Patterned paper, stickers (Pebbles); metal label holder (Jo-Ann Stores); letter stamps (PSX Design); photo turns (7 Gypsies); distress ink (Ranger); solvent ink (Tsukineko); pen

NOT SO TOUGH

A rough and tough exterior encases the heart of a gentleman, as Julie expresses in this playful page dedicated to her husband's softer side. She distressed the edges of the design with chalk ink to add to the rugged appearance. The ribbon with stitching lends just a hint of heartwarming charm and illustrates the journaling with authenticity.

Supplies: Patterned papers (Me & My Big Ideas); textured cardstock (Prism Papers); sticker (Sweetwater); wooden letters (Westrim); rub-ons (Memories Complete); wooden tag (Go West Studios); mini brad (Queen & Co.); ribbon (K & Company); chalk ink (Clearsnap)

NOT SO TOUGH

AUTHENTIC
the real thing

American Original

ROUGH & RUGGED R ROUGH & RUGGED

I describe you as a tough guy. Your look, your style, but to me your not so tough. The way you touch my hand, the smile on your face, the way you took Hayden into your arms the day he was born. You walk the walk, and talk the talk, but underneath it all, your a gentle man.
—unique

Julie Johnson, Seabrook, Texas

MY HUSBAND...

Donna decided to dedicate a scrapbook to her groom while on her honeymoon, which was when this photo of her husband was taken. She gave the page a Southwestern flair reminiscent of their Las Vegas/Arizona vacation by first painting over a canvas frame. Donna then wrapped wooden letters around the frame and covered the brads throughout the page with stickers. A printed canvas accent and coordinating ribbons continue the look and feel of the patterned paper.

Supplies: Patterned papers, western stickers (Flair Designs); textured cardstocks (Bazzill); rub-on letters (Autumn Leaves); canvas frames, canvas phrases, wooden letters (Li'l Davis Designs); button (Westrim); ribbon, rickrack (Making Memories, May Arts); brads

Kenny:
Yes, you are my everything. You entered my life and made me smile at a time in which I felt like crying - I'm still full of those smiles. Because of your patience, selflessness, and loving, gentle nature, I've become a better person with you by my side - I'm not as self-centered as I used to be. For countless other reasons, you are my world, and that will never change.

Donna M. Bryant, North Attleboro, Massachusetts

CAPTURE MY HEART

A timeless love that never grows old is celebrated on Summer's page that commemorates her relationship with her best friend and love. She created her own unique embellishments by cutting shapes from the patterned paper with a craft knife and layering her photos beneath the edges. A journaling tag is tucked inside a stamped envelope.

Supplies: Patterned paper (Daisy D's); printed transparency (Creative Imaginations); slide mount (DMD); metal heart snaps, spiral clip (Making Memories); word charm (All My Memories); fiber (Great Balls Of Fiber); letter stamps (Stampin' Up!); walnut ink (Ranger); cardstock; vintage lace

Summer Ford, Bulverde, Texas

Ryan..You are my confidant and my best friend. I love your smile, it lights up my life. I love your heart, it makes me feel so loved. I love being in your presence. You are my number one fan. When I am with you, I feel like a queen and that together we can conquer anything. You have captured my heart.

YOUR LAUGHTER

Glenni's husband is one of the funniest men she knows, and she designed this layout as a gift to show her appreciation for the joy he endlessly and effortlessly brings to their home. Subtle machine-stitching, subdued, coordinating ribbons and staples provide understated design touches, while tags dangling from safety pins and jump rings provide a gleam of silver to attract the eye.

Supplies: Patterned papers (Basic Grey); rub-on letters (Autumn Leaves, Making Memories); metal-rimmed tags (Jo-Ann Stores); safety pins (Making Memories); letter stamps (Li'l Davis Designs, Making Memories, Technique Tuesday); ribbon (Michaels); solvent ink (Tsukineko); metal charm (source unknown); pen

Glenni Light, Plymouth, Massachusetts

SAM

Sherrill designed this page to celebrate her friend Sam after swapping photos in a scrapbooking group (they called the process "Trading Faces!"). The bright blues, festive browns and cheerful patterns are quieted with the use of a stitched canvas pocket reminiscent of a man's shirt. Sherrill accented the pocket and right corners with a decorative stamp and used coordinating rub-on title letters for her page title.

Supplies: Patterned papers, printed transparency (KI Memories); foam letter stamps (Making Memories); rub-on letters (Creative Imaginations); canvas pocket (source unknown); cardstock; ribbon; acrylic paint; stamping ink

Sherrill Ghilardi Pierre, Maplewood, Minnesota

MY FOREVER AUTUMN LOVE

Kim Turpin, Victoria, British Columbia, Canada

The art of self-sacrifice in the interest of a loved one is a gift that Kim's husband readily bestows. She designed this crisp and cool layout to show her appreciation for all the autumn walks he has accompanied her on for the sheer reason of making her smile. Kim kept the design simple by layering and stitching together two autumn-toned papers. Matted block stickers accented with ribbons add a playful touch.

Supplies: Patterned papers (Basic Grey, Karen Foster Design); textured cardstock (Bazzill); letter stickers (American Crafts, Rusty Pickle); dictionary strip sticker (Pebbles); printed twill (Junkitz); ribbon, rub-on letters (Making Memories); rub-on word (Kopp Design); mini spiral clip (Creative Imaginations); square punch (EK Success); thread

TO WALK IN THESE SHOES

Upon receiving a new camera, Jen immediately began snapping photographs at random of items around her home. The image of her husband's shoes left Jen wondering what she would ever do without him, which set into motion the creation of this tribute that pays homage to the irreplaceable traits and talents he lovingly shares with his family. Leather frames, maroon ribbons and warm, rich colors lend a masculine dignity to the page.

Supplies: Patterned papers (Family Archives, Hot Off The Press, Mustard Moon, 7 Gypsies); bottle cap, bottle cap stickers (Mustard Moon); letter stickers (Pebbles); ribbon (May Arts); leather frame (Making Memories); stamping ink

Jen Nichols, Orland, Indiana

Christine's younger brother is an aspiring rock star with the talent and dedication to make the dream a reality. She designed this two-page spread to encourage him to relentlessly pursue his goals and dreams. The warm reds and yellow in Christine's color scheme were drawn from the desert backdrop in the photographs, accentuating the rays of the sun on his face. The distressed look of the cut title letters also cater to the hues and textures captured in the artful image.

Supplies: Patterned papers (Autumn Leaves, Designs by Reminisce, Karen Foster Design); leather pieces (Rusty Pickle); brads (Making Memories)

Christine Brown, Hanover, Minnesota

THE GOOD STUFF

A Kenny Chesney country hit with the same title inspired this layout, which Julie felt compelled to create at 3:00 in the morning! She included her husband's rugged photo along with a distressed image of his vintage car, adding her own lyrics to describe the "good stuff" in life by printing on patterned paper. The aged look of the "antiques" sticker perfectly complements the throwback feel of the page, helping to prove the best things in life are the classics, much like Julie's husband.

Supplies: Patterned papers (Li'l Davis Designs, 7 Gypsies); ribbon (SEI); sticker (Karen Foster Design); definition tab (Autumn Leaves); chalk ink (Clearsnap); staples

AUTHENTIC

[ə-'then-tik] Aa

the good stuff

The smell of a newborn baby
Kisses from Hayden
The way she loves me
Little handprints on the window
Hangin' with good friends
The smell of sunshine after the rain
A tall glass of sweet tea
Momma's fried chicken
The sound of a child's laughter
A dip in the pool on a hot summer day

ANTIQUES

Julie Johnson, Seabrook, Texas

MY HUSBAND MATT

Kent's husband is such an integral part of her life that she actually created this page as part of her all-about-me album. She combined patterned papers and printed vellum to enhance her message of how much better, richer, brighter and more fun her life is because he is in it. A spiral heart clip attached to a corrugated paper strip holds together a mini album of sepia-toned images of Matt in action, as husband, father—Kent's true love.

Supplies: Patterned paper (Amscan); printed vellum (EK Success); heart clip (ScrapArts); photo corners (Canson); tags (DMD); cardstock; corrugated paper; fibers

Kent Nichols, San Jose, California

I think my husband Matt can do anything. You may not believe me but after being married to someone for ten years and watching him be able to pick up any instrument and play, examine any antique and tell you where it originated, who made it and how much it is worth, or decipher the current political arena you may begin to see it my way. He is a rock and a man of unwavering faith. He always gives people second chances and never holds grudges. I can always depend on his calm personality. He has a sense of humor so I never know what to expect and I get lots of practice rolling my eyes. Most of all he is a loving husband and father. The joy that he gives me without even knowing when he is playing around with the boys or telling me he loves me for the "umpteenth" time makes me glad to be alive and part of his life.

ADDITIONAL INSTRUCTIONS AND CREDITS

Cover

It doesn't get much more manly than this. Torrey created her texture-rich design using such hardware store finds as paint, corrugated cardboard, ball chain, keys, nuts, paint chips and laminate samples. Self-adhesive foam spacers add eye-appealing elevation while metal mesh-mounted, paint-treated journaling commemorates an enduring friendship.
Torrey Scott, Thornton, Colorado
Photos: Allison Orthner, Calgary, Alberta, Canada

Supplies: Hinge sticker (Creek Bank Creations); conchos (Scrapworks); nameplate (Magic Scraps); ruler sticker (EK Success); rub-on letters (Making Memories); cardstock; transparency; acrylic paint; brads; cardboard; ball chain; nuts; postal scale; cloth; keys; laminate chips; paint chips

P. 3 Book plate

Torrey's assemblage all but screams garage work-space glam. Painted corrugated cardboard, paint chips, a faux hinge and measuring tape make for a manly masterpiece mounted on boldly colored cardstock. Blueprint patterned paper and ball chain strung with faux keys add a dimensional element.
Torrey Scott, Thornton, Colorado

Supplies: Hinge stickers (Creek Bank Creations); key stickers (EK Success); rub-on letters (Making Memories); cardstock; cardboard; acrylic paint; paint chips; brads; ball chain

P. 7 Paul

Jodi captures the essence of her dear friend with deep colors and rich textures. A template was used to create the eye-catching zigzag page borders which were "popped" with self-adhesive foam spacers for dimension. Jodi added a little elevation to the first letter of her page title in the same fashion for extra flair.
Jodi Amidei, Memory Makers Books
Photos: Torrey Scott, Thornton, Colorado

Supplies: Patterned paper (Scenic Route Paper Co.); specialty paper (K & Co.); template (Cut It Up); cardstock; stamping ink; self-adhesive foam spacers

P. 8 . . .Talking With a Scrapbook Widower
Amy Goldstein, Kent Lakes, New York

Supplies: Patterned paper (Imagination Project); textured cardstock (Bazzill); brads (Junkitz)

P. 8 Q&A
Shannon Taylor, Bristol, Tennessee

Supplies: Patterned paper, tag (Rusty Pickle); chipboard words (Li'l Davis Designs); chipboard letters (Heidi Swapp); square brads (Karen Foster Design); ball chain (Pebbles); jump rings (Junkitz); eyelets (Creative Impressions); color wash (Ranger); cardstock

P. 9 Daddy's Girl
Heather Preckel, Swannanoa, North Carolina

Supplies: Patterned papers (Imagination Project, 7 Gypsies); textured cardstock (Bazzill); buttons, letter buttons (Junkitz); woven label (Scrapworks); staples; brads

P. 9 Morning Routine
Courtney Walsh, Winnebago, Illinois

Supplies: Patterned papers, rub-on words, cardstock sticker (Chatterbox); textured cardstock (Bazzill); buttons (Junkitz); white letter stickers (American Crafts); black letter stickers (Making Memories); date stamp (Office Max); ribbon; stamping ink

P. 10 Mr. Fix It

Tons of textures and fix-it-man flair celebrate the pride Sheila feels toward her mechanic/pilot/writer/and now home inspector. A stone-textured paint gives the look of sandpaper to her title letter stencil and balances the soft effect of the letters textured with suede paint. She wrapped copper wire around a title letter for thematic effect and to coordinate with the metal-stamped copper and washer. Screw heads, black mesh and electric tabs perfectly accent the photos and finish the handyman look of the layout.
Sheila Doherty, Couer d'Alene, Idaho

Supplies: Patterned papers (7 Gypsies, Chatterbox, Daisy D's, Karen Foster Design, KI Memories, Scenic Route Paper Co.); textured cardstock (Prism Papers); mesh (Magic Mesh); copper wire, washers, electric tabs, copper (Scrappin' Ware); metal stamps (Pittsburgh); chipboard letters, embroidery floss, screw heads (Making Memories); suede textured spray paint, stone textured spray paint (Krylon); walnut ink (Ranger); cardstock

P. 10 How Bad Do You Want It?

You can almost hear the engines revving and smell the hot tires and blacktop burning on Christina's page that is dedicated to her hubby's horse-powered hobby. Distressed black-and-white checkered paper mimics the look of a racing flag while staggered journaling strips with a slightly "singed" look evoke a sense of heat. Christina kept her creative wheels turning by calling upon license plate letter stickers and stencil numbers to continue her race car-inspired design and used lyrics from a song by Tim McGraw for the perfect page title.
Christina Husk, Deer Park, Washington

Supplies: Patterned papers (Creative Imaginations, Wordsworth); stickers (Sticker Studio) label maker (Dymo); cardstock; stencils; ribbon; stamping ink; eyelets; staples

P. 11 Gift of Love

This image of little Justin with his grandpa is one of Ivette's favorite photos, and she gave it a home on this page that celebrates just what it means to have such a special male role model. Ivette scanned, enlarged and printed the photo onto vellum to give it a soft and timeless quality and drew from its colors to give the page an earthy, outdoorsy and laid-back feel. Wooden letters, corrugated paper and ribbons lend texture and depth to this tranquil and treasured moment.
Ivette Valladares, Miami Lakes, Florida

Supplies: Patterned papers (Chatterbox, K & Company); letter stickers (K & Company); wooden letters (Li'l Davis Designs); mini brads, metal label holder, colored safety pins (Making Memories); buttons (Chatterbox); corrugated paper (DMD); hemp; ribbons; sandpaper; poem (www.twopeasinabucket.com)

P. 11 Success

While furthering his education, Alecia's husband was asked to write an essay on "success" in one of his university classes. Alecia printed portions of the essay on a transparency and swiped portions of the back with acrylic paint to provide artful journaling blocks around the page perimeters. She took this photo the same day he went back to school as a way to document his personal and academic growth.
Alecia Ackerman Grimm, Atlanta, Georgia

Supplies: Patterned paper, letter stickers (Basic Grey); distress ink (Ranger); transparency; acrylic paint

P. 12

Supplies: Patterned papers (Creative Imaginations, Karen Foster Design, Leisure Arts); stencils (Autumn Leaves, Heidi Swapp); office supplies (Autumn Leaves, Colorbok, Design Originals, Dymo, EK Success, Making Memories); mesh (Magic Mesh, Making Memories); hardware (Memories in the Making/Leisure Arts); paint chips (Lowe's)

P. 13

Supplies: Patterned papers (EK Success, Karen Foster Design, Paper House Productions) auto accents (Sticker Studio); leather (EK Success, Making Memories); bottle caps (Design Originals); woven labels and sentiments (Junkitz, Me &My Big Ideas); laminate chips (Lowe's)

P. 14

Supplies: Patternd papers (Karen Foster Design, Leisure Arts, Paper House Productions); watch parts (vintage/found); metal (EK Success, Karen Foster, KI Memories, Making Memories); game pieces (Li'l Davis Designs, ScrapArts, 7 Gypsies); wood (Chatterbox, Lara's Crafts, Li'l Davis Designs); mailbox letters and numbers (Making Memories)

P. 15

Supplies: Patterned papers (EK Success, Karen Foster Design) chipboard (Li'l Davis Designs); buttons (Rusty Pickle, found); die cuts (Paper House Productions); stickers (Me & My Big Ideas, Paper House Productions, Sticker Studio); printed sentiments (Chatterbox)

SOURCE GUIDE

The following companies manufacture products featured in this book. Please check your local retailers to find these materials, or go to a company's Web site for the latest product. In addition, we have made every attempt to properly credit the items mentioned in this book. We apologize to any company that we have listed incorrectly, and we would appreciate hearing from you.

3L CORPORATION
(800) 828-3130
www.scrapbook-adhesives.com

7 GYPSIES
(800) 588-6707
www.7gypsies.com

ADOBE SYSTEMS INCORPORATED
(866) 766-2256
www.adobe.com

ALL MY MEMORIES
(888) 553-1998
www.allmymemories.com

ALL NIGHT MEDIA
(see Plaid Enterprises)

ALL SORTS OF THINGS- no contact info

AMERICAN ART CLAY CO. (AMACO)
(800) 374-1600
www.amaco.com

AMERICAN CRAFTS
(801) 226-0747
www.americancrafts.com

AMERICAN TAG COMPANY
(800) 223-3956
www.americantag.net

AMERICAN TRADITIONAL DESIGNS®
(800) 448-6656
www.americantraditional.com

AMSCAN, INC.
(800) 444-8887
www.amscan.com

ANIMA DESIGNS
(800) 570-6847
www.animadesigns.com

ANNABEL'S ALBUM- no contact info

ARCSOFT®, INC.
(510) 440-9901
www.arcsoft.com

AUTUMN LEAVES
(800) 588-6707
www.autumnleaves.com

BASIC GREY™
(801) 451-6006
www.basicgrey.com

BAZZILL BASICS PAPER
(480) 558-8557
www.bazzillbasics.com

BLUMENTHAL LANSING COMPANY
(201) 935-6220
www.buttonsplus.com

BO-BUNNY PRESS
(801) 771-4010
www.bobunny.com

BOXER SCRAPBOOK PRODUCTIONS
(503) 625-0455
www.boxerscrapbooks.com

BROTHER® INTERNATIONAL CORPORATION
www.brother.com

CANSON®, INC.
(800) 628-9283
www.canson-us.com

CARD CONNECTION- see Michaels

CAROLEE'S CREATIONS®
(435) 563-1100
www.ccpaper.com

CAVALLINI PAPERS & CO., INC.
(800) 226-5287
www.cavallini.com

CHARTPAK
(800) 628-1910
www.chartpak.com

CHATTERBOX, INC.
(208) 939-9133
www.chatterboxinc.com

CLEARSNAP, INC.
(360) 293-6634
www.clearsnap.com

CLOUD 9 DESIGN
(763) 493-0990
www.cloud9design.biz

CLUB SCRAP™, INC.
(888) 634-9100
www.clubscrap.com

COLORBÖK™, INC.
(800) 366-4660
www.colorbok.com

CRAF-T PRODUCTS
(507) 235-3996
www.craf-tproducts.com

CRAFTS, ETC. LTD.
(800) 888-0321
www.craftsetc.com

CREATIVE IMAGINATIONS
(800) 942-6487
www.cigift.com

CREATIVE IMPRESSIONS RUBBER STAMPS, INC.
(719) 596-4860
www.creativeimpressions.com

CREATIVE MEMORIES®
(800) 468-9335
www.creativememories.com

CREEK BANK CREATIONS, INC.
(217) 427-5980
www.creekbankcreations.com

CROSSED PATHS™
(972) 393-3755
www.crossedpaths.net

CROSS-MY-HEART-CARDS, INC.
(888) 689-8808
www.crossmyheart.com

C-THRU® RULER COMPANY, THE
(800) 243-8419
www.cthruruler.com

DAISY D'S PAPER COMPANY
(888) 601-8955
www.daisydspaper.com

DARICE, INC.
(800) 321-1494
www.darice.com

DELUXE DESIGNS
(480) 497-9005
www.deluxedesigns.com

DENAMI DESIGN RUBBER STAMPS
(253) 437-1626
www.denamidesign.com

DESIGN ORIGINALS
(800) 877-0067
www.d-originals.com

DESIGNS BY REMINISCE
(319) 358-9777
www.shopreminisce.com

DIANE'S DAUGHTERS®
(801) 621-8392
www.dianesdaughters.com

DIECUTS WITH A VIEW™
(877) 221-6107
www.dcwv.com

DIGITAL SCRAPBOOK PLACE, THE
(866) 396-6906
www.digitalscrapbookplace.com

DMD INDUSTRIES, INC.
(800) 805-9890
www.dmdind.com

DOODLEBUG DESIGN™ INC.
(801) 966-9952
www.doodlebug.ws.

DUNCAN ENTERPRISES
(800) 782-6748
www.duncan-enterprises .com

DYMO
www.dymo.com

EK SUCCESS™, LTD.
(800) 524-1349
www.eksuccess.com

EMAGINATION CRAFTS, INC.
(866) 238-9770
www.emaginationcrafts.com

FAMILY ARCHIVES™, THE
(888) 622-6556
www.heritagescrapbooks.com

FAMILY TRADITIONS- no contact info

FANCY PANTS DESIGNS, LLC
(801) 779-3212
www.fancypantsdesigns.com

FIBERMARK
(802) 257-0365
http://scrapbook.fibermark.com

FIBERS BY THE YARD™
(405) 364-8066
www.fibersbytheyard.com

FINDINGS AND THINGS- no contact info

FISKARS®, INC.
(800) 950-0203
www.fiskars.com

FLAIR® DESIGNS
(888) 546-9990
www.flairdesignsinc.com

FONTWERKS
(604) 942-3105
www.fontwerks.com

FOOFALA
(402) 330-3208
www.foofala.com

GOTTA MESH™/NOTIONS MARKETING
(616) 243-8424
www.gottamesh.com

GOTTA SCRAP!, INC.
(972) 772-5197
www.gottascrapgottastamp.com

GO WEST STUDIOS
(214) 227-0007
www.goweststudios.com

GRAFIX®
(800) 447-2349
www.grafix.com

GREAT BALLS OF FIBER
(303) 697-5942
www.greatballsoffiber.com

HAMPTON ART STAMPS, INC.
(800) 229-1019
www.hamptonart.com

HEADLINE- no contact info

HEIDI GRACE DESIGNS
(866) 89heidi
www.heidigrace.com

HEIDI SWAPP/ADVANTUS CORPORATION
(904) 482-0092
www.heidiswapp.com

HERO ARTS® RUBBER STAMPS, INC.
(800) 822-4376
www.heroarts.com

HOME DEPOT U.S.A., INC.
www.homedepot.com

HOT OFF THE PRESS, INC.
(800) 227-9595
www.paperpizazz.com

IMAGINATION PROJECT, INC.
(513) 860-2711
www.imaginationproject.com

JAQUARD PRODUCTS/RUPERT
GIBBON & SPIDER, INC.
(800) 442-0455
www.jacquardproducts.com

JENN'S SANITY- no contact info

JHB INTERNATIONAL
(303) 751-8100
www.buttons.com

JO-ANN STORES
(888) 739-4120
www.joann.com

JOY CO.- no contact info

JUDIKINS
(310) 515-1115
www.judikins.com

JUNKITZ™
(732) 792-1108
www.junkitz.com

K & COMPANY
(888) 244-2083
www.kandcompany.com

KAREN FOSTER DESIGN
(801) 451-9779
www.karenfosterdesign.com

KI MEMORIES
(972) 243-5595
www.kimemories.com

KOPP DESIGN
(801) 489-6011
www.koppdesign.com

KRYLON®
(216) 566-200
www.krylon.com

LACEY PAPER CO.- no contact info

LA PLUMA, INC.
(803) 749-4076
www.debrabeagle.com

LARA'S CRAFTS
(800) 232-5272
www.larascrafts.com

LASTING IMPRESSIONS FOR PAPER, INC.
(801) 298-1979
www.lastingimpressions.com

LEAVE MEMORIES
www.leavememories.com

LI'L DAVIS DESIGNS
(949) 838-0344
www.lildavisdesigns.com

LOERSCH CORPORATION USA
(610) 264-5641
www.loersch.com

LOWE'S COMPANIES, INC.
(800) 44-LOWES
www.lowes.com

LUMINARTE (formerly Angelwing Enterprises)
(866) 229-1544
www.luminarteinc.com

MAGENTA RUBBER STAMPS
(800) 565-5254
www.magentastyle.com

MAGIC MESH
(651) 345-6374
www.magicmesh.com

MAGIC SCRAPS™
(972) 238-1838
www.magicscraps.com

MAKING MEMORIES
(800) 286-5263
www.makingmemories.com

MAKIN'S CLAY®/SINO HARVEST LIMITED
www.makinsclay.com

MARA-MI, INC.
(800) 627-2648
www.mara-mi.com

MA VINCI'S RELIQUARY
http://crafts.dm.net/
mall/reliquary/

MAY ARTS
(800) 442-3950
www.mayarts.com

MCGILL, INC.
(800) 982-9884
www.mcgillinc.com

ME & MY BIG IDEAS®
(949) 883-2065
www.meandmybigideas.com

MELISSA FRANCES/HEART & HOME, INC.
(905) 686-9031
www.melissafrances.com

MEMORIES COMPLETE™, LLC
(866) 966-6365
www.memoriescomplete.com

MEMORIES IN THE MAKING/LEISURE ARTS
(800) 643-8030
www.leisurearts.com

MEMORIES IN UNIFORM
(757) 228-7395
www.memoriesinuniform.com

MEMORY CREATORS
www.memorycreators.com

MICHAELS® ARTS & CRAFTS
(800) 642-4235
www.michaels.com

MICROSOFT CORPORATION
www.microsoft.com

MOMENTS DEFINED, INC.
(866) 910-4366
www.momentsdefined.com

MOREX CORPORATION
(717) 852-7771
www.morexcorp.com

MRS. GROSSMAN'S PAPER
Company
(800) 429-4549
www.mrsgrossmans.com

MUSTARD MOON™
(408) 299-8542
www.mustardmoon.com

MY MIND'S EYE™, INC.
(800) 665-5116
www.frame-ups.com

NRN DESIGNS
(800) 421-6958
www.nrndesigns.com

OFFICE DEPOT
www.officedepot.com

OFFICE MAX
www.officemax.com

OFFRAY
(800) 344-5533
www.offray.com

OUTDOORS & MORE SCRAPBOOK DECOR
(801) 390-6919
www.outdoorsandmore.com

PAPER ADVENTURES®
(800) 525-3196
www.paperadventures.com

PAPER HOUSE PRODUCTIONS
(800) 255-7316
www.paperhouseproductions.com

PAPER LOFT
(866) 254-1961
www.paperloft.com

PAPER LOVE DESIGNS
(510) 841-1088
www.paperlovedesigns.com

PEBBLES INC.
(801) 224-1857
www.pebblesinc.com

PITTSBURGH- no contact info

PIXIE PRESS
(888) 834-2883
www.pixiepress.com

PLAID ENTERPRISES, INC.
(800) 842-4197
www.plaidonline.com

PRISM™ PAPERS
(866) 902-1002
www.prismpapers.com

PROVO CRAFT®
(888) 577-3545
www.provocraft.com

PRYM-DRITZ CORPORATION
www.dritz.com

PSX DESIGN™
(800) 782-6748
www.psxdesign.com

QUEEN & CO./THE EYELET QUEEN
(858) 485-5132
www.eyeletqueen.com

QUICKUTZ, INC.
(801) 765-1144
www.quickutz.com

RANGER INDUSTRIES, INC.
(800) 244-2211
www.rangerink.com

RHONNA FARRER- no contact info

RIVER CITY RUBBER WORKS
(877) 735-2276
www.rivercityrubberworks.com

ROYAL BRITES
(800) 669-7692
www.royalbrites.com

RUBBER STAMPEDE
(800) 423-4135
www.deltacrafts.com

RUSTY PICKLE
(801) 746-1045
www.rustypickle.com

SAKURA HOBBY CRAFT
(310) 212-7878
www.sakuracraft.com

SARAH BOND- no contact info

SARAH HEIDT PHOTO CRAFT, LLC
(734) 424-2776
www.sarahheidtphotocraft.com

SCENIC ROUTE PAPER CO.
(801) 785-0761
www.scenicroutepaper.com

SCRAPARTS
(503) 631-4893
www.scraparts.com

SCRAPGOODS™ (a division of The Scrap Pack)
www.scrapgoods.com

SCRAPPING WITH STYLE
(704) 254-6238
www.scrappingwithstyle.com

SCRAPPIN' WARE- no contact info

SCRAPWORKS, LLC
(801) 363-1010
www.scrapworks.com

SCRAPYARD 329
(775) 829-1118
www.scrapyard329.com

SEI, INC.
(800) 333-3279
www.shopsei.com

SIZZIX®
(866) 742-4447
www.sizzix.com

STAMPABILITIES®
(800) 888-0321
www.stampabilities.com

STAMP DECOR- no contact info

STAMPINKS UNLIMITED
www.stampinks.com

STAMPIN' UP!®
(800) 782-6787
www.stampinup.com

STICKER STUDIO™
(208) 322-2465
www.stickerstudio.com

SWEETWATER
(800) 359-3094
www.sweetwaterscrapbook.com

SWIBCO, INC.
(630) 968-8900
www.swibco.com

TANDY LEATHER COMPANY
(800) 433-3201
www.tandyleather.com

TARGET
www.target.com

TECHNIQUE TUESDAY, LLC
(503) 644-4073
www.techniquetuesday.com

TEXTURED TRIOS- no contact info

TSUKINEKO®, INC.
(800) 769-6633
www.tsukineko.com

USARTQUEST, INC.
(517) 522-6225
www.usartquest.com

WAL-MART STORES, INC.
(800) WALMART
www.walmart.com

WARNER- no contact info

WESTRIM® CRAFTS
(800) 727-2727
www.westrimcrafts.com

WORDSWORTH
(719) 282-3495
www.wordsworthstamps.com

INDEX